PETER COKER

1926-2004

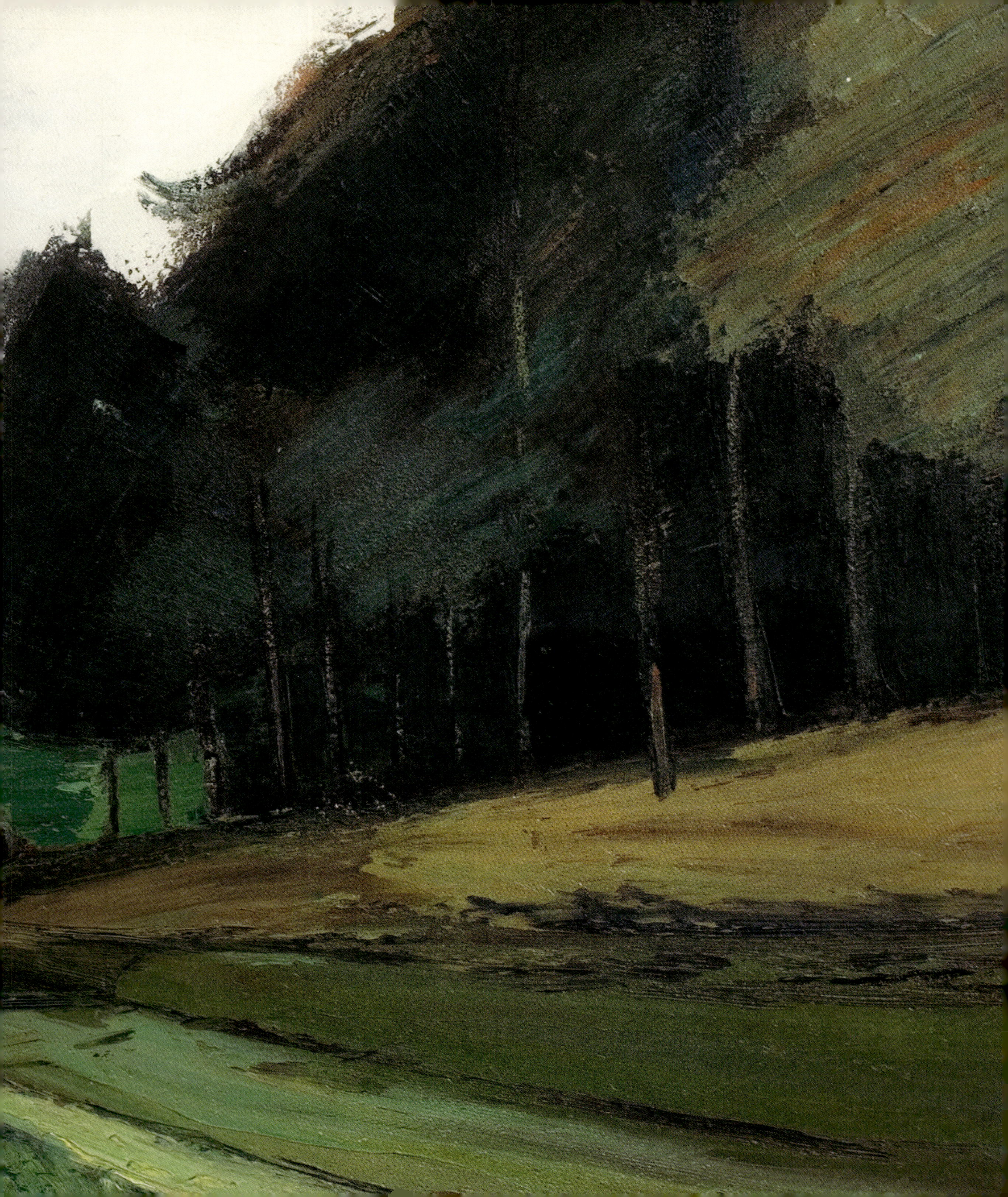

PETER COKER

MIND AND MATTER

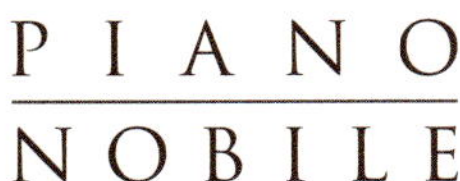

PIANO NOBILE | ROBERT TRAVERS WORKS OF ART LTD

129 Portland Road | London W11 4LW | +44 (0)20 7229 1099

info@piano-nobile.com | piano-nobile.com

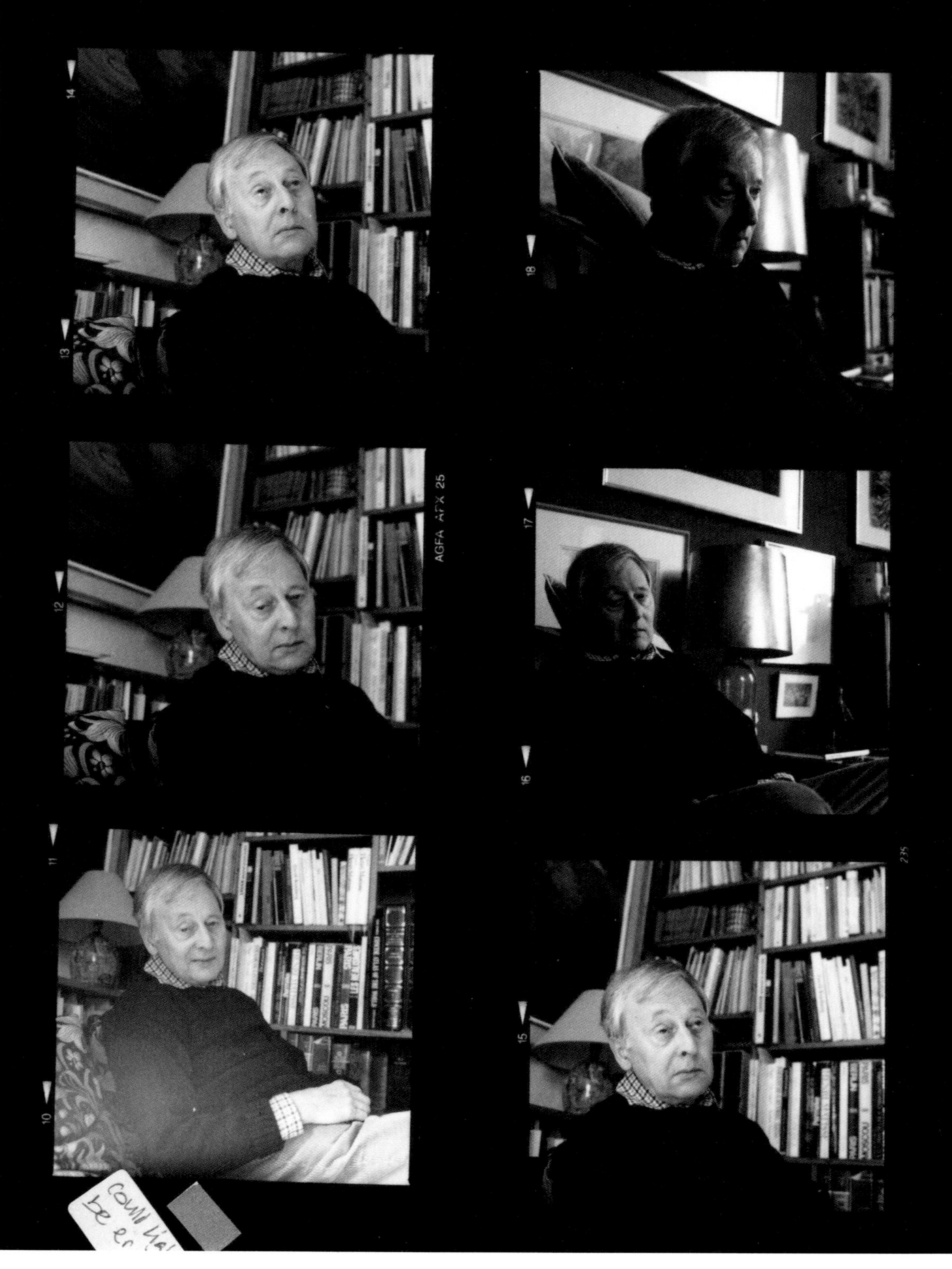

CONTENTS

PIANO
NOBILE

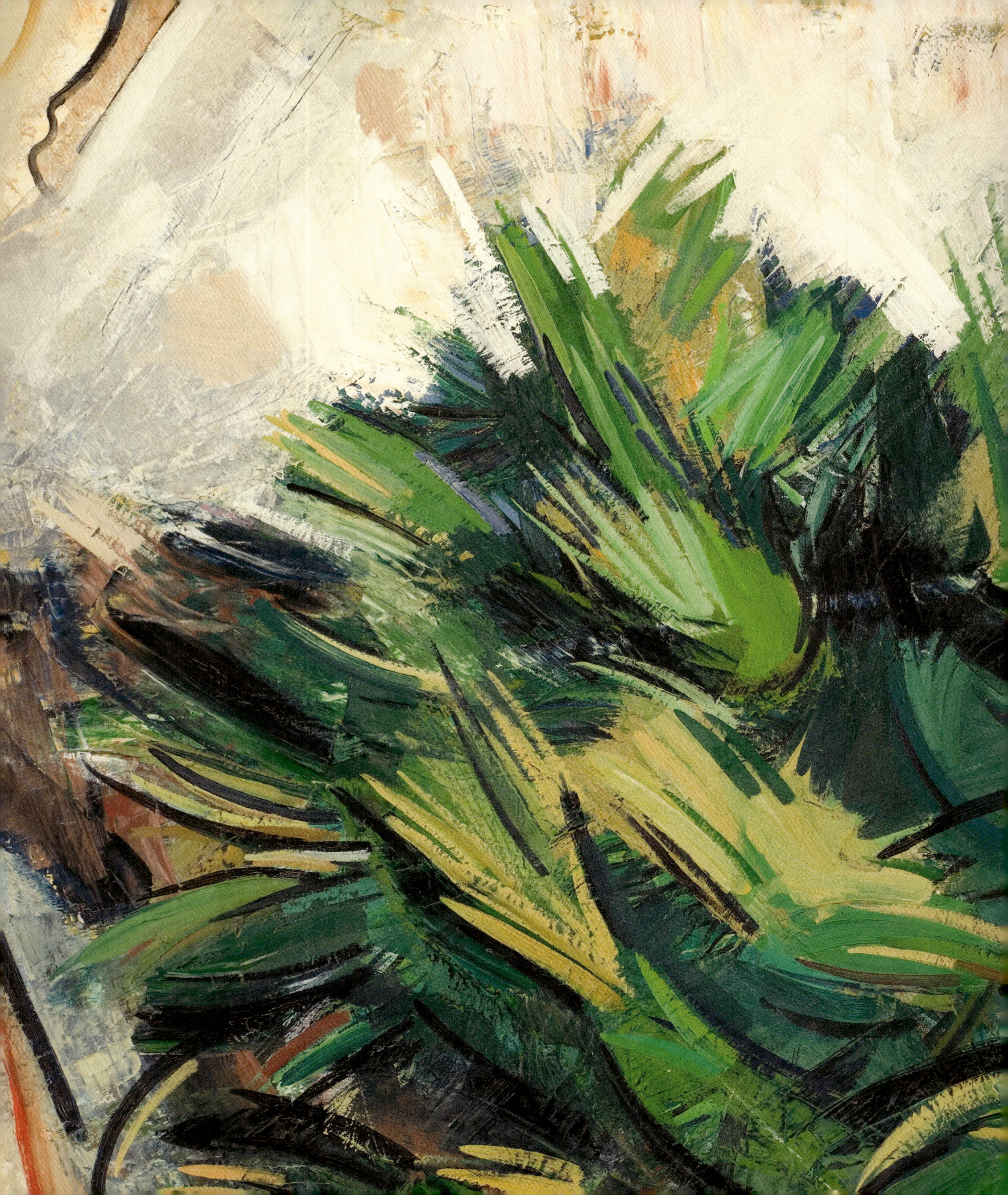

PETER COKER: ARTIST AND STOIC

I only got to know Peter Coker well following his son and my friend Nicholas's untimely death in 1985. We had first met for a meal in Paris in about 1977 when we were all attending exhibitions and visiting museums there, a regular part of Peter's life. France was in many respects Peter's artistic and spiritual home. I think I was an important living connection for Peter and his wife Vera with their lost son. We also got on very well and I was always fascinated to listen to Peter talking about his favourite art and about the making of paintings.

I frequently visited Peter and Vera at their Essex home, The Red House, in Mistley, near the River Stour which forms the border with Suffolk - real painters' country. It was a handsome square, red-brick, early nineteenth century building with a well-tended garden, a high-ceilinged sitting room with large windows nearly to the floor. Peter's studio was upstairs. It was light and tidy with canvases stacked in rows and brushes, paints, and other materials and equipment, neatly ordered and ready to hand. It reminded me of a craftsman's workshop, quite the opposite in its unassuming calmness to the chaos of, say, Francis Bacon's famous studio in South Kensington. Peter would have disappointed anyone hoping to meet a disturbing genius; he was fastidious in everything and entirely unpretentious in his manner, not at all the Soho type. He was born in East London, but from ordinary Leytonstone, not picturesque Whitechapel.

Peter and Vera were generous hosts and took their cooking very seriously, buying meat via mail from the best West Country farms. A favourite dish was a whole salmon cooked to perfection and served with a few fresh local vegetables. There was always an excellent bottle of French wine on the table. Peter loved literature and history and read widely and with great deliberation, carefully considering each sentence for sense and effect. Lunchtime discussion would often focus on a particular writer or topic and, as with art, Peter focused on the meaning and structure of words. I have perhaps over-stressed his seriousness; Peter and Vera laughed loudly and frequently and found humour in all areas of life.

I would say that Peter was a natural Stoic. He faced the world, its events and the things he painted, with a steady gaze, finding order and moments of beauty where possible and accepting that which is simply there or cannot be controlled. From the very beginning of his career, Peter's painting was a finely balanced attempt to express a measured feeling of joy in a world which so often resists that effort.

Richard Humphreys

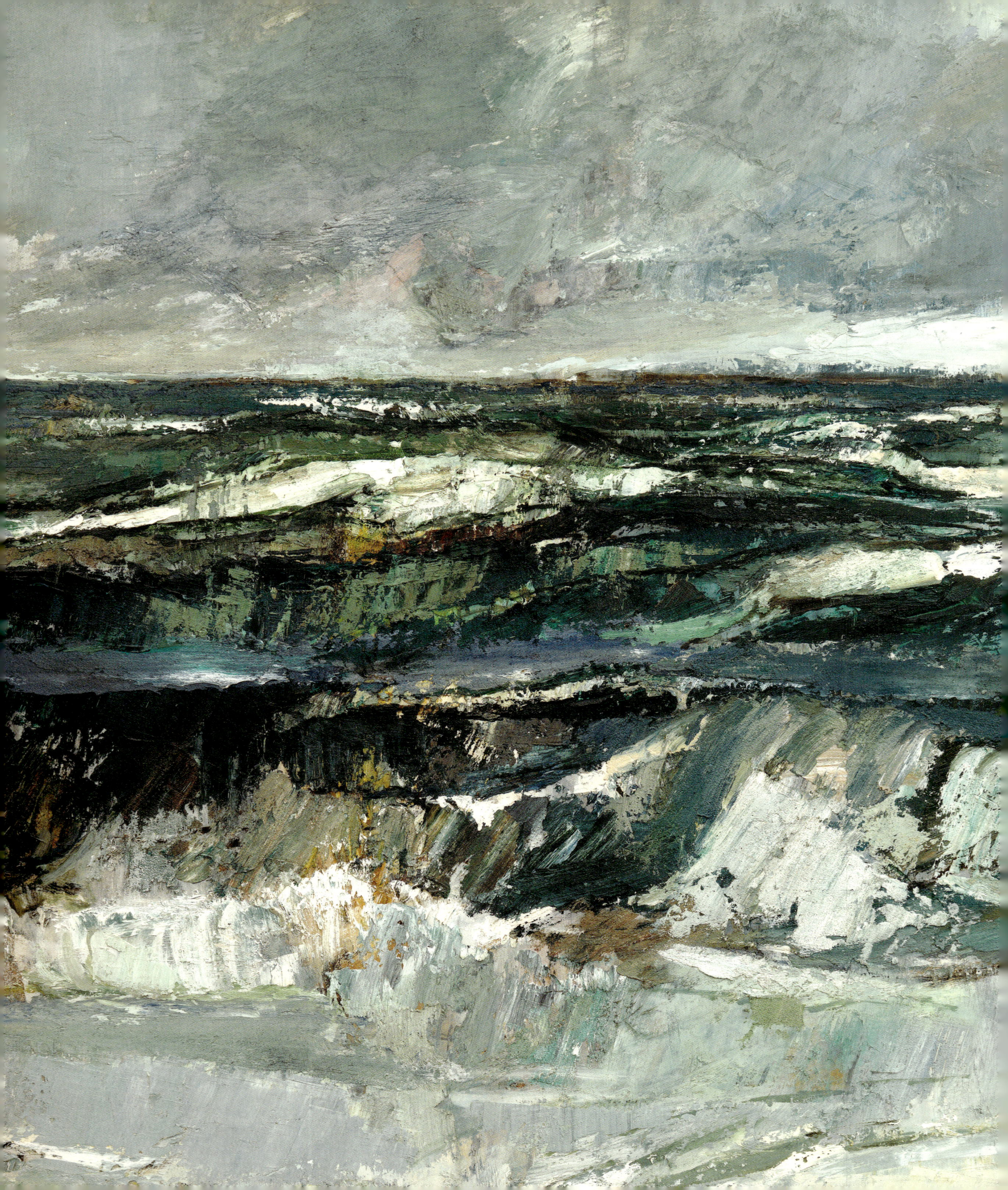

On 16 March 1955, Franco-Russian artist Nicolas de Staël threw himself to his death from the terrace of his apartment in Antibes, on the Côte d'Azur in France. A few days later, Peter Coker set out from London to venture on his first trip to France beyond the city limits of Paris. Travelling by train and bus, Coker intended the journey as modern-day pilgrimage to Gustave Courbet, the nineteenth-century French Realist painter. Following in Courbet's footsteps, the Barbizon and Fontainebleau forests and the town of Étretat on the Normandy coast were the sites earmarked by Coker to pay homage to the great master who would turn out to be the most significant influence on his career. The tour was conducted in the shadow of de Staël's death: violent endings entwined with the nascent flourishing of Coker's enduring affinity for the French landscape.

Speaking in an interview in 1989, Coker self-consciously positioned himself within the trajectory of art history: "it's not only a search for identification but also feeling one's part of the tradition. I don't know if I could ever have made a move without coming into contact with exhibitions in the late 1940s and early 1950s at the National Gallery."[1] Situating himself and his work within a lineage of artists that stretched from Courbet through Cézanne and culminating in de Staël, with notable additions to this trio, Coker insisted on the significance of artistic inheritance. In stark contrast, he rejected any attempts to claim him for defined contemporary movements, most notably the so-called 'Kitchen Sink' group in the mid-1950s: "I kept on my own, going my own way."[2] The emphasis of the vertical axis surpassed the influence of the lateral.

Whilst artistic ancestors shaped his creative life, his personal life was touched by the tragedy of losing of his only child, Nicholas Coker, in 1985. Nicholas was arguably the most sensitive writer on his father's work, introducing the catalogue for Coker's 1979 touring exhibition of paintings and drawings from the Butcher's Shop period with an eloquence and insight near unmatched. An art historian by training, Nicholas Coker's concern was with elucidating his father's work for posterity.

As Coker cast his eye back over history to mine antecedents, his gaze came to rest primarily upon French characters – he was a committed Francophile for most of his life – but a handful of British artists completed the cast. The encounter between Coker and these historical forerunners occurred, almost without exception, at definitive locations. Influence was filtered through the specificity of place as Coker toured the sites favoured by the artists he revered. Coker was too talented an artist to mimic, but with acute sensitivity and perception, his vision of the world was constantly altered by the art that touched him, and, correspondingly, his mode of depiction was subject to an ever-persistent evolution. In Coker's words: "I think when you see exhibitions...you challenge your own thoughts, you refurbish the mind and eye, you are remoulded."[3]

Peter Coker was born on 27 July 1926, the only child of Elsie and Edwin Coker. Despite the reluctance of his father, Coker enrolled at St Martin's School of Art and the Central School of Art in 1941, before serving first in the Fleet Air arm and then the Education Corps during World War II. Upon being de-mobbed in 1947, Coker undertook full-time studies at St Martin's until 1950, continuing his studies until 1954 at the Royal College of Art. He was a somewhat solitary figure at art college, close to his teachers Vivian Pitchforth and James Stroudley at St Martin's and Rodrigo Moynihan at the RCA but removed from the hubbub of student life. His first solo exhibition in 1956 at the Zwemmer Gallery, attached to the Zwemmer bookshop, propelled him into the public sphere garnering critical attention for his drawings and paintings of animal carcasses hanging from the hooks in his local butcher's shop. The unbridled realism of Coker's works and their simultaneous exaltation of the working-class trade of butchery was hailed by John Berger, the Marxist art critic. Coker was immediately associated with the Kitchen Sink group – John Bratby, Edward Middleditch, Derrick Greaves and Jack Smith – though Coker continued to show with Zwemmer Gallery whilst the other four were exhibited by Helen Lessore's Beaux Arts gallery.

It was landscape that would be the dominant theme of Coker's career, a subject that he found invigorating and stimulating. Travelling through France and, closer to home, East Anglia, his lifelong muses revealed themselves in the guise of dense woodlands and dramatic coastlines. Coker was elected an Associate Royal Academician in 1965 and a full Academician in 1972; the institution played an important role in Coker's life socially and professionally, and he exhibited frequently in the Summer Exhibition. Serious health issues plagued Coker's life but his drive to travel and to paint overcame physical trials. With an interlude in the 1990s, Coker painted throughout his life and almost right up to his death in 2004.

***

The earliest, and longest-standing, influence upon Coker was also the first in the lineage, the maverick Realist and occasional revolutionary Gustave Courbet (1819-1877). Courbet's masterpiece, *A Burial at Ornans*, 1949-50, was a touchstone for Coker throughout his career; Coker frequently returned to view the work in the flesh in the Musée d'Orsay for creative replenishment. At the heart of *A Burial at Ornans*, and Coker's pictures of butchery, lies a concern with ritual. Life, and death, of the ordinary man becomes worthy of a tragic epic through the consolatory aggrandisement bestowed by ritual. In his Butcher's Shop works, particularly those depicting the butcher himself such as *Man Carrying Pig*, 1955; Tate, Coker glorifies the strength and skill of the working-class tradesman. Coker uncovers something spiritual, even religious, in the actions and aesthetics of butchery.

Echoing the labour of the trade Coker painted, his own working process required immense physicality and drew attention to materiality. James Hyman has argued that the morality of the 1950s was writ into the very methods and materials artists employed: "bold use of paint would become a leitmotif of social realism with thick-paint carrying workman-like associations in contrast to *belle peinture*."[4] Using a palette knife, huge slabs of impasto paint were dragged to and fro across wooden boards, sometimes until the paint slid off the backing under its own weight.

Coker's veneration of Courbet was a somewhat unusual focus amongst his peers. For young artists, the influence of Paul Cézanne (1839-1906), the unrivalled master of modernity, still held sway. Coker could not but respond to Cézanne's inescapable and pervasive legacy – he did prove to be a formative presence in Coker's youth but as an artist whose work Coker determined to consciously reject. Whilst still-life was a genre that was important to Coker throughout his student days, he purposefully avoided the prosaic subject matter found in Cézanne's works of apples and lemons spilling over cloth-covered rickety tables in cafes in provincial France. This resolve to exchange the traditional for the shocking led him to an East London butcher's shop.

The next descendant in Coker's family tree of artistic inheritance, Vincent Van Gogh (1853-1890), spoke positively and powerfully to Coker's sensibilities and, in turn, to his choice of subject matter. Van Gogh was the receipient of a major exhibition at the Tate in 1948 and it seems more than likely that Coker first encountered the Dutch artist here. Van Gogh's revelation of the spiritual within his environs - the mysticism of a star-scattered night, the potential of an empty chair, the portent of crows suspended over a wheat-field – find their equivalence in Coker's landscapes. Introducing Coker's touring retrospective exhibition in 1972, Frederick Gore wrote, "he sees landscape not as the microcosm of an ordered universe but as a play of forces...at some times as immensely stable and at others as alarmingly precarious. Our recognition of this order and chaos is partial, inadequate, partly in our own minds. Accepting this, he paints both the comforts and terrors that our environment offers, with equal curiosity."[5] Coker's three iterations of *Sunflowers*, 1958-59 [cat. 7], offer the most rudimentary connection between Van Gogh and Coker: it is not subject matter so much as vision that link the two. A genealogy can be drawn between the symbolism that blossomed in Van Gogh's landscapes and still-lifes, and the tumultuous life and death forces that Coker confronted in every tree or wave or cliff-face.

It was the last in the lineage, however, that impelled Coker into the realm of the modern. The life and art of Nicolas de Staël, the Russian artist claimed by the French avant-garde, achieved a notoriety of tragic, near-mythic proportions. Depressed and increasingly isolated in the final years of his life, de Staël killed himself following a discouraging meeting with an art critic. The shadow cast by de Staël upon Coker and his contemporaries was deep. The Matthiesen Gallery hosted a seminal exhibition of de Staël's work in 1952 followed by a posthumous retrospective at the Whitechapel gallery in 1956. The presence of de Staël, the enduring spectre of his paintings, permeates both Coker's vision and his process.

Like de Staël, Coker rejected *en plein air* painting in place of sketches done in situ and worked up into paintings in the studio. A cyclical working method emerged in Coker's practice, whereby he gained sustenance from encountering the great outdoors on a substantial trip every few months and retreated to the studio to bring these locations to life in oil paint before returning for rejuvenation, to 're-energise' in his words, by working outside.[6] Likewise his travels adopted a tautological pattern. Coker tended to spurn unknown territory, revisiting old haunts – these beloved spots were general historically frequented by the artists he admired. Inspiration resided not just in the landscape but in the knowledge that an artistic idol had previously chanced upon wells of creativity in the same vicinity. Nowhere was this more evident for Coker than in Audierne and Antibes, coastal towns where de Staël had been based.

Coker's relationship with place was complex, with layers of meaning built into each locale. His relationship with time was equally multifaceted. Unmistakably, he felt the weight of history as he grappled with each picture but also with the eternal dichotomy for a figurative artist between the momentary and the permanent. With every painting that addressed the elements of sun, wind, water and earth, Coker sought to transform a fleeting and transitory experience into painted form

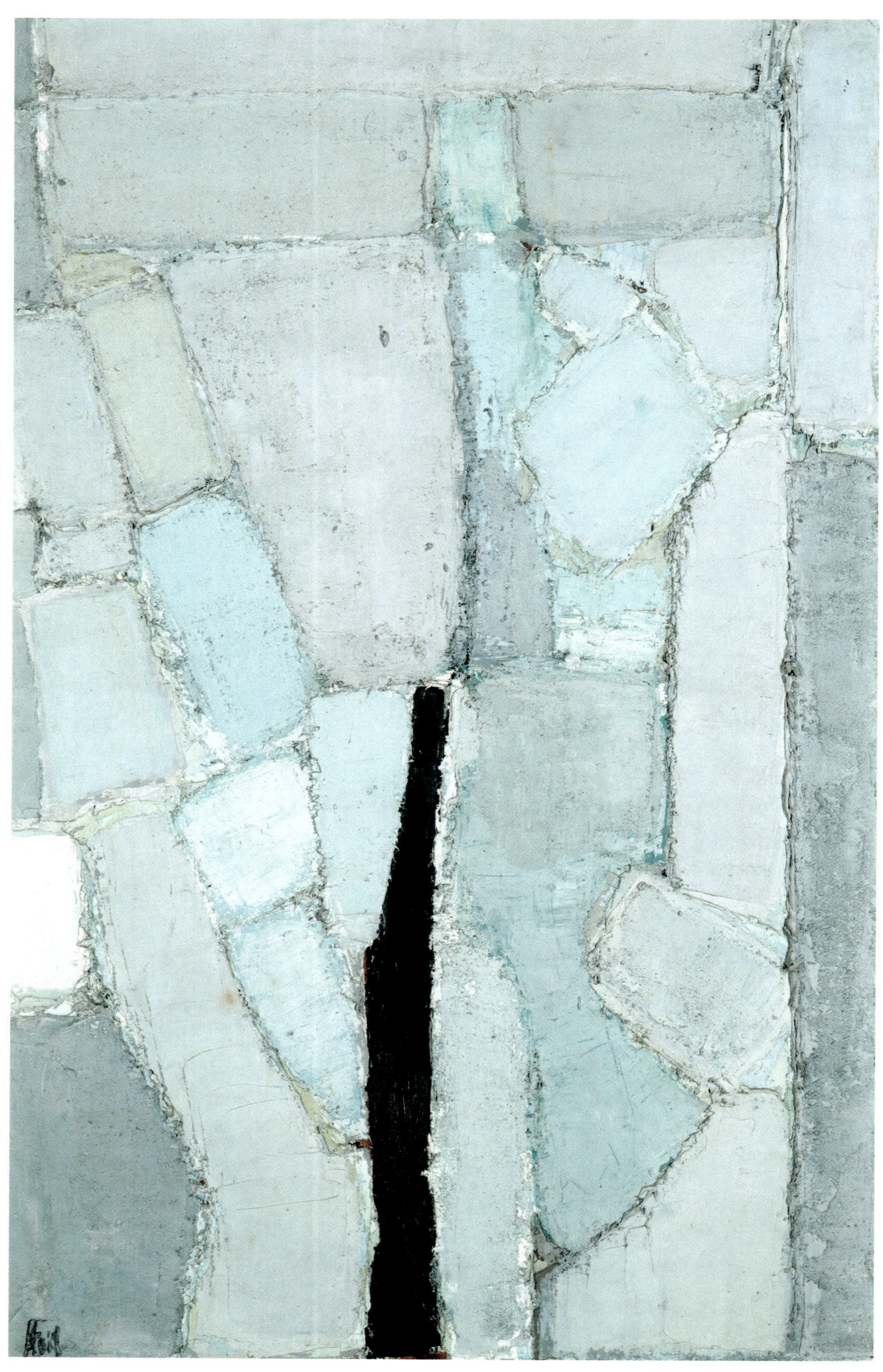

Fig. 1 Nicolas de Staël (1914 – 1955)
Composition 1950, 1950 Tate, London

for posterity. De Staël famously stated that he was "an impaler of things that life offers to me as it passes by." Coker elided the instantaneous with movement: "I think that one thing that's always been a very big part of my work is movement, to which is linked my own emotional and technical vitality."[7]

The materiality of de Staël's paintings was undoubtedly the catalyst behind Coker's similar manipulation of paint by the mid-1950s. The physicality of the method was integral to its success: "I always believe that it's out of the process of painting that everything is generated."[8] Slabs of impasto paint were applied by Coker with a palette knife, moulded, smoothed, scrapped and plastered onto board supports over lead white, a putty-like ground. Layer upon layer of oil paint was hauled over the surface, breaking and cracking to reveal substrata. Sparse, dry and crumbling passages contrasted with thick, luscious and smooth swathes. Coker's paintings during the 1950s and early 1960s possessed a tactility that is simultaneously seductive and transgressively modern. Paint metamorphosed into an object, battling with the subject matter for primacy and indeed the material often obscured rather than elucidated the subject it described.

Closer to home, affinities between Coker and the 'School of London' artists are often underplayed, not least by Coker himself, but Coker should be considered in the great figurative tradition of post-war painting in Britain. Francis Bacon's depictions of raw meat were important precursors for Coker's Butcher's Shop scenes; Michael Andrews's stalking scenes and predilection for expansive panoramas offer a parallel to Coker's landscapes. Similarities abound between Coker's use of paint and the almost contemporary work of Leon Kossoff and Frank Auerbach, with whom Coker would have overlapped at both St Martin's and the RCA. The weight of the paint was a visual manifestation of the intensity of feeling and the depth of scrutiny ascribed by both artists to the process of painting the urban landscape of London and its inhabitants. Evidently, Coker lived a life far removed from the Colony Club but his works are palpably of the post-war zeitgeist.

Coker claimed the father-figures for the 'School of London' as formative influences: "I think I'm very much a part of the strong tradition of the 1950s, that rather low-toned painting based on Sickert and Whistler. They are artists that have never ceased to interest me."[9] Coker painted a tribute to another of these forefathers, John Singer Sargent, in 1986, *Homage to John Singer Sargent (The Daughters of Edward D Boit)*, itself, in turn, an emulation of Diego Velaźquez's *Las Meninas*. Here, Coker's lineages intersect: Whistler, Sickert's mentor, was a student of Courbet. The presence of Whistler and Sickert re-surfaces with the second phase of Coker's career, in his shift in emphasis to the environs of southern France. Replacing the grey skies and wild seas of Normandy for the dazzling light and verdant scenery of the Mediterranean, Coker developed a particular preoccupation with the transition between interior and exterior. A series of scenes exploring thresholds, the stark contrast between a murky room and bright midday sun are redolent of Whistler and Sickert's interiors. Coker's move to the south of France, consciously or otherwise, followed a well-trodden path. De Staël but also Matisse, Picasso, Bonnard and Van Gogh all spent their final years under the glow of the Mediterranean sun in France. Though Coker was drawn to the Mediterranean for its own sake, once there, its previous residents had to be faced in his painting.

Though consciously assuming the mantle inherited from an illustrious tradition of realist and landscape painters, Coker fashioned it in a vigorously modern guise. Too-long famed for his earliest work at the expense of a thorough assessment of his career in its totality, Coker cultivated a truly distinctive balance of the cerebral and the material. He was an artist of intellect and of instinct.

Ferndale, Rhondda, 1952

Titled and dated lower right 'Ferndale
S. Wales Rhondda Valley
April 10th 52'
Gouache on paper
56.3 × 38.2 cm | 22⅛ × 15⅛ in

Provenance
Private Collection, UK

Exhibitions
1954, London, The Piccadilly Gallery, *Exhibition of Contemporary Watercolours*, no. unknown [rediscovered work].

During the Easter break of his second year at the Royal College of Art, Peter Coker travelled to South Wales at the invitation of his college football teammate, Colin Allen, a student in the Department of Graphic Design. Coker was seeking inspiration for the large scale painting each student was required to produce by the end of the second year of studies. Over the course of his trip in April 1952, Coker visited a different colliery every day, reaching the sites by bus, to a total of around a dozen drawings. These works were the last to be formulated *en plein air*. In conversation with Andrew Lambirth in 1989, Coker recollected: "During my second year I began to concentrate a lot on still-life, but I also began to feel that the imaginative side of my work was not really developing. I went to Wales, working out of doors in the mining district...After that I started to rely on working from drawings. This was a crucial development... After College it was a question of trying to learn to use my drawings in relation to my paintings and to find a way of collecting the material, finding a system of notation that I could read when back at the studio."[10] Working from drawings, rather than from life, facilitated an artistic freedom unburdened from fidelity to the scene before his eyes and rather led by innate creativity, rooted in but not chained to reality.

This trio of gouache on paper works, *Ferndale, Rhondda*, *Ystrad, Rhondda*, and *Dowlais Steel Works, Cardiff*, all 1952, form part of the Wales set that also includes two further examples now in the collection of the National Museum Wales. Two scenes look down over the Rhondda Valley, following the sweep of peaks and vales enveloping the mines, whilst the third surveys the plain of the East Moors with rail tracks leading to the Dowlais Works. Whilst it would be easy to read an underlying socio-political message into these works - the young student depicting the industrial heartlands of South Wales – Coker was adamant that such interpretation was baseless. Responding to politically-charged readings of his Butcher's Shop phase, but equally relevant for the Welsh works, Coker stated: "For me, there was no political or social significance to what we were doing, one just worked on material one found interesting. I kept on my own, going my own way."[11]

Coker's interest primarily resides in capturing the effervescent effects of smoke and steam, emitted in a mass of plumes punctuating the industrial vistas. Seeking to express the transient and immaterial spirals hanging in the valleys in painted form, Coker scumbles gouache in white and grey over near monochrome scenes. Paradoxically for an artist associated with monumentality, solidity and heavily worked impasto, Coker argued that "one thing that's always been a big part of my work is movement, to which is linked my own emotional and technical vitality."[12] In the Welsh works, Coker attempts not to cement but to convey the fleeting and the ever-changing trails of smoke. Though Coker could never have predicted, these works now represent a compelling historical record of an obsolete industry and a bygone landscape.

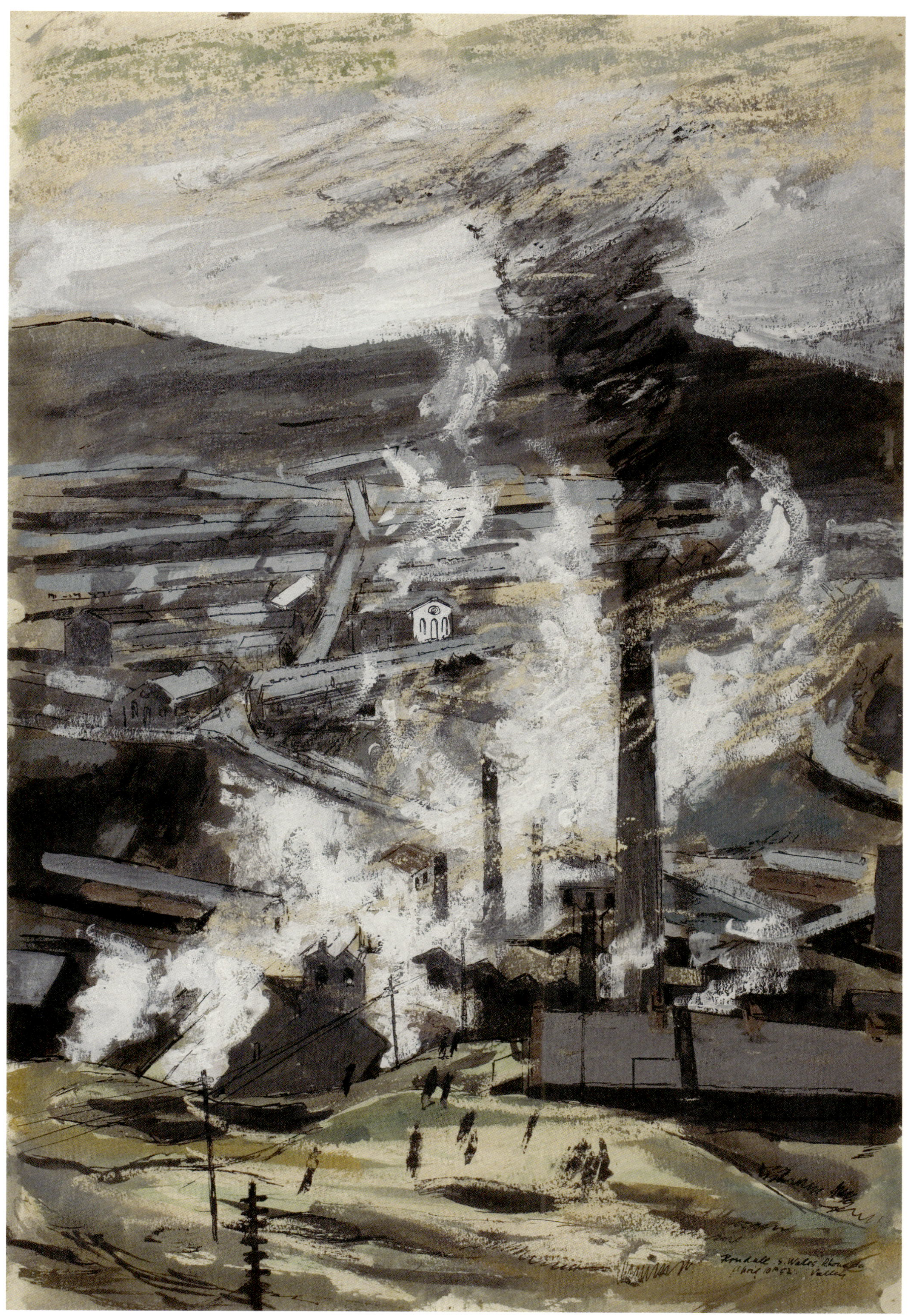

Ystrad, Rhondda, 1952

Titled and signed lower right 'S. Wales
April 12th 52 Ystrad Rhondda'
Gouache on paper
37.6 × 55.4 cm | 14¾ × 21¾ in

Provenance
Private Collection, UK

Literature
David Wootton with contributions by John Russell
Taylor and Richard Humphreys, *Peter Coker RA*
(Chris Beetles Ltd, 2002), cat. rais. no. 25, p. 117.

Exhibitions
1954, London, The Piccadilly Gallery, *Exhibition of
Contemporary Watercolours*, no. 11.

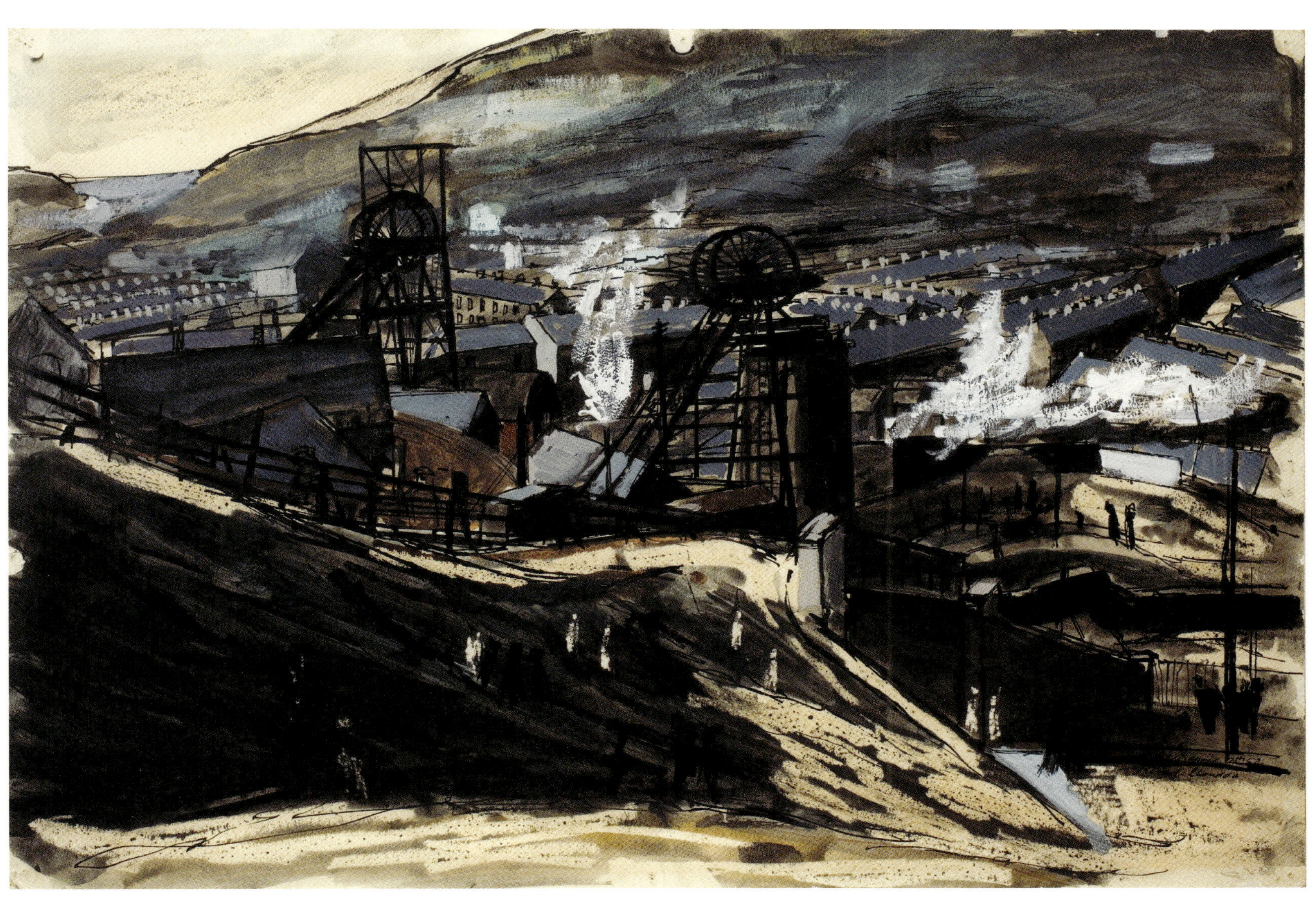

Dowlais Steel Works, Cardiff, 1952

Titled and dated 'Steel works smoke Cardiff
April 52 Dowlais Works'
Gouache on paper
38.5 × 56.7 cm | 15⅛ × 22⅜ in

Provenance
Private Collection, UK

Literature
David Wootton with contributions by John Russell
Taylor and Richard Humphreys, *Peter Coker RA*
(Chris Beetles Ltd, 2002), cat. rais. no. 18, p. 117
[listed as *Dowlas Steel Works, Cardiff*].

Exhibitions
1954, London, The Piccadilly Gallery, *Exhibition of
Contemporary Watercolours*, no. 9.

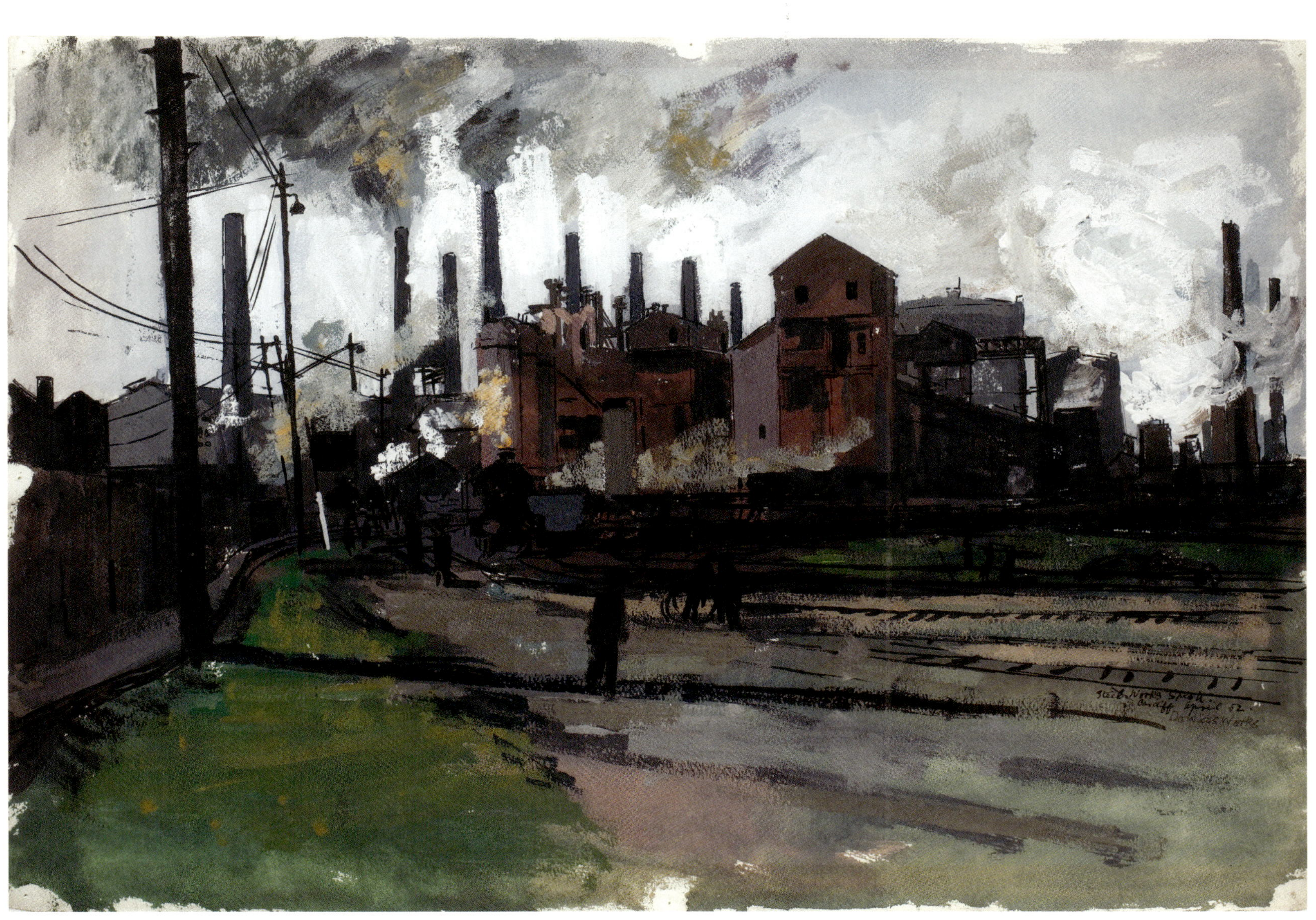

4

Dead Hare, c.1955

Signed lower right 'Peter Coker'
Charcoal on board
73.5 × 53.2 cm | 29 × 21 in

Povenance
Caroline Steane

Literature
A. Lambirth and C. Etter, *A monographic
exploration of Peter Coker's 1958-9 'Sunflowers'*
(Piano Nobile Publications, 2012), col. ill. p. 4.

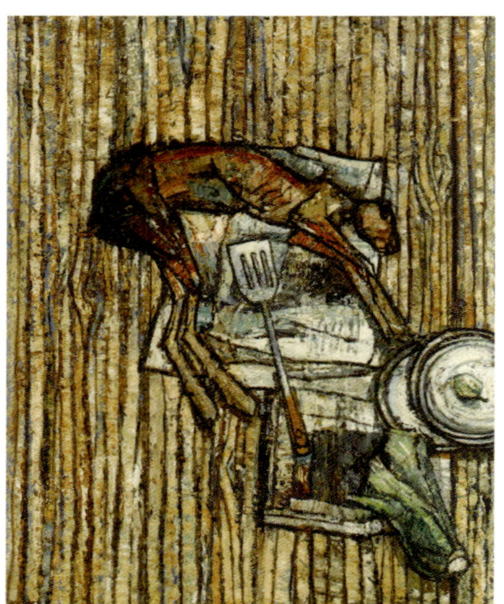

Fig. 2, Peter Coker, *Dead Hare on Table*, 1955
Arts Council Collection, Southbank Centre, London

During his final year at the RCA, Coker fixed upon the subject that evolved into the material for his first solo exhibition at Zwemmer Gallery in 1956, featuring drawings and paintings of animal carcasses, obsessively rendered in impasto oil. The show propelled him to fame alongside fellow realists John Bratby, Jack Smith, Derrick Greaves, and Edward Middleditch, who were all exhibited by Helen Lessore at the Beaux Arts gallery. Reluctant recipients of the Kitchen Sink Group title, a phrase coined by critic David Sylvester, the group were lauded by Marxist critic John Berger for finding valour in the everyday. From 1954, Coker began to introduce carcasses of animals into his art, drawing from life either at his local butcher's or purchasing pig and deer heads, rabbits, and fish, which he laid out on a grainy wooden bench to use as subject matter. Distancing himself from the legacy of Cézanne's still-lifes, Coker instead consciously aligned himself with the morbid realism of Chaïm Soutine, whose work he probably saw at an exhibition in Paris at Galérie Weil in 1953.

The ritual of butchery has parallels with Coker's emphasis on the physicality of the very act of painting: "I always believe that it's out of the process of painting that everything is generated."[13] Introducing Coker's touring retrospective 1972-73, Frederick Gore wrote, "Perhaps the aim of all ritual is to show that pain or cruelty of life is subject to a moral order…the pleasures of the eye and the enjoyment of very lavish and sumptuous paint have to be shaped, even at great labour, into a design which firmly embraces the essentials and not the accidents of the subject."[14]

In 1955, Coker produced a series of dead hares, including this work, *Dead Hare*, and three oils shown at his 1956 Zwemmer Gallery exhibition: *Dead Hare on Table*, Arts Council Collection [Fig. 2], *Still Life with Hare and Grapes*, Chelmsford Museum, and *Still Life with Hare*, Tullie House Museum and Art Gallery. Unlike the skinned example in *Dead Hare on Table*, *Dead Hare* illustrates the hare intact, a perfect specimen, untouched by signs of death, laid out on a table. Working in charcoal, Coker focuses on the lush texture of fur and the taut, elongated muscles of the hare's powerful hind legs. Although ostensibly a still-life, the macabre subject of a dead hare was designed to shock, to repulse, to force the still-life genre joltingly into modernity.

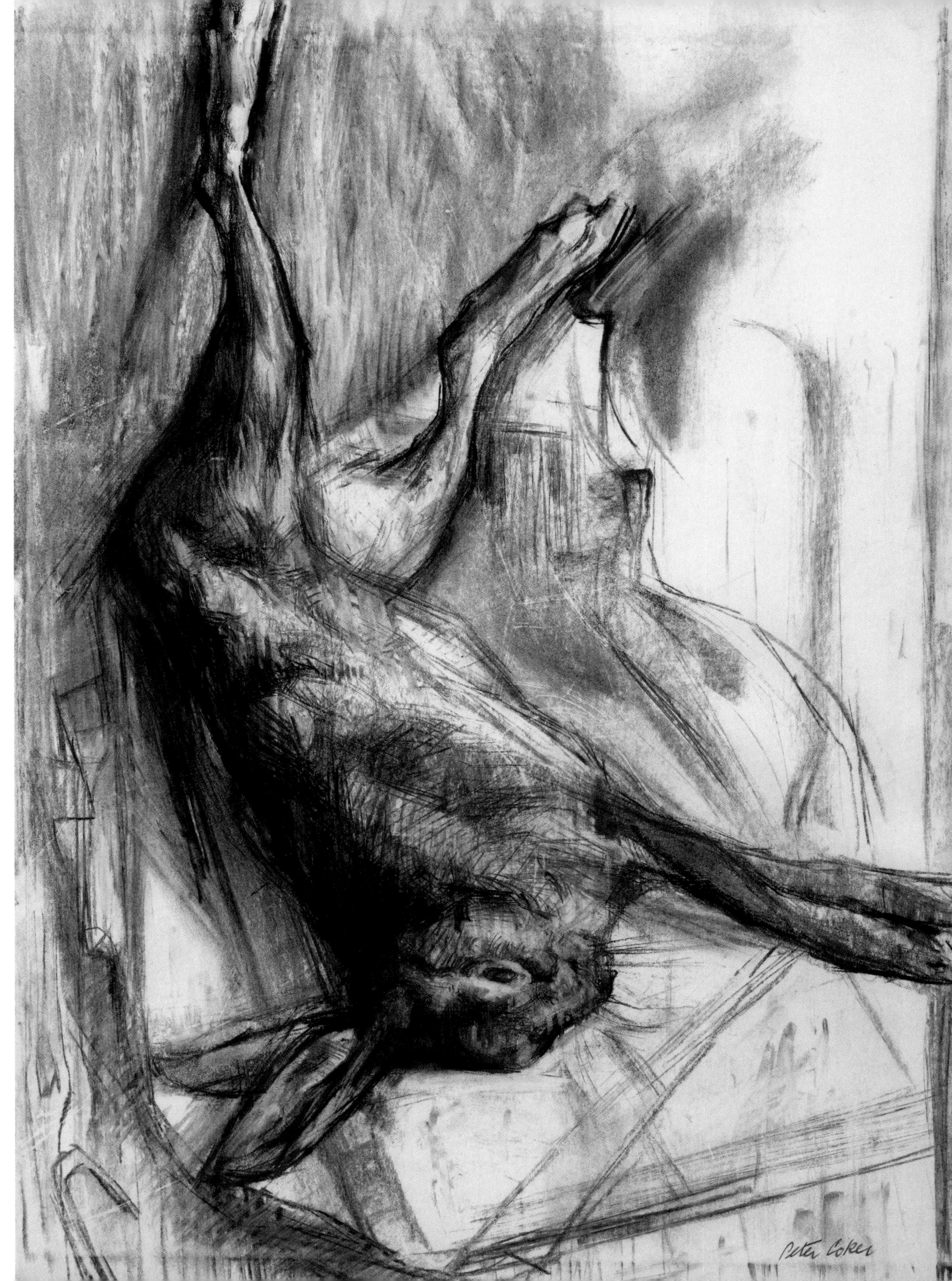

Peter Coker

5

Still Life with Fish, 1957

Signed lower left 'Peter Coker'
Oil on hardboard
120 × 79 cm | 47¼ × 31⅛ in

Provenance
Zwemmer Gallery
Private Collection
Julian Hartnoll
The Maas Gallery, London, 13 June 2003
The Stanley J. Seeger Collection
Private Collection, UK

Literature
David Wootton with contributions by John Russell
Taylor and Richard Humphreys,
Peter Coker RA (Chris Beetles Ltd, 2002), cat. rais.
no. 64, p. 119, col. ill., p. 119.

Exhibitions
1959, London, Zwemmer Gallery, *Peter Coker*, no. 1.

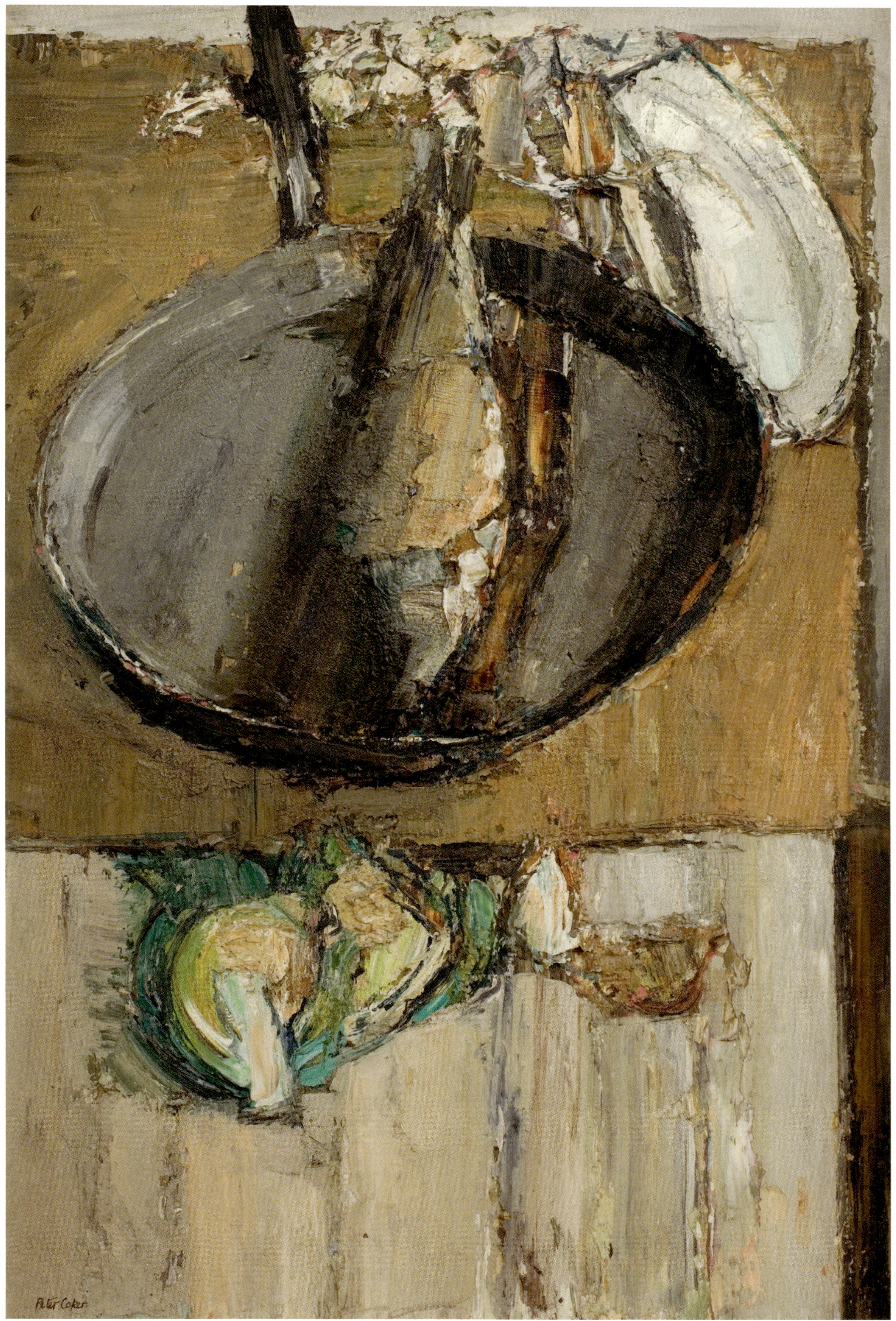
Peter Coker

Still Life with Fish, 1957, was exhibited at Peter Coker's third solo exhibition with the Zwemmer Gallery in 1959, one of only two still-life oils in an exhibition dominated by landscapes. On Coker's usual grainy wooden table, a black frying pan holds a whole fish, probably a mackerel, with a handful of vegetables including a cauliflower and garlic scattered across the table top. Coker has alighted upon the domesticity of a meal in progress, a brief pause as ingredients are prepared but cooking not yet begun. The extraordinary angle of *Still Life with Fish*, so that the table top is parallel to that of the picture plane, was formulated in reality by Coker: "I worked from drawings, finding much greater imaginative freedom, lifting the tables up (inclining the plane by propping up the back legs) creating the impetus for particular distortions."[15]

An exhibition in 1979 at the Royal Academy, that toured the UK, presented Coker's Butcher's Shop works as a distinct and potent part of his oeuvre. The catalogue was introduced by Coker's son, Nicholas, who emphasised the significance of texture to the oils: "Texture is important, a smooth slab of paint for example, becomes our sense of a roll of fat. The tactile quality of the images is due to this kind of correspondence, and is part of an attempt to make the form more real." The immensely dense impasto paint laid over lead white applied to the board support takes on a near sculptural quality. Coker continues: "In that the painting is made as a reality, ultimately independent of the subject, the thickness of the paint attains to the objective reality formerly associated with the shape of the object."[16] As well as depicting the form of the still-life, the painting adopts the substance of the objects within the still-life, laying claim to its own objectivity through the sheer weight of its materiality.

Still Life with Fish was acquired by Stanley J. Seeger, the prominent American collector, to hang above his bed in Sutton Place, reportedly replacing a Francis Bacon triptych. It is one of the last remaining examples of Coker's Kitchen Sink Group works to remain in private hands with the majority held in public collections including *Sheep Carcasses on a Bench*, 1955; Royal Academy of Arts, *Man Carrying Pig*, 1955; Tate, *Table and Chair* (featuring Nicholas Coker as a child), 1955; Tate, and *Butcher's Shop No. 1*, 1955; Museums Sheffield.

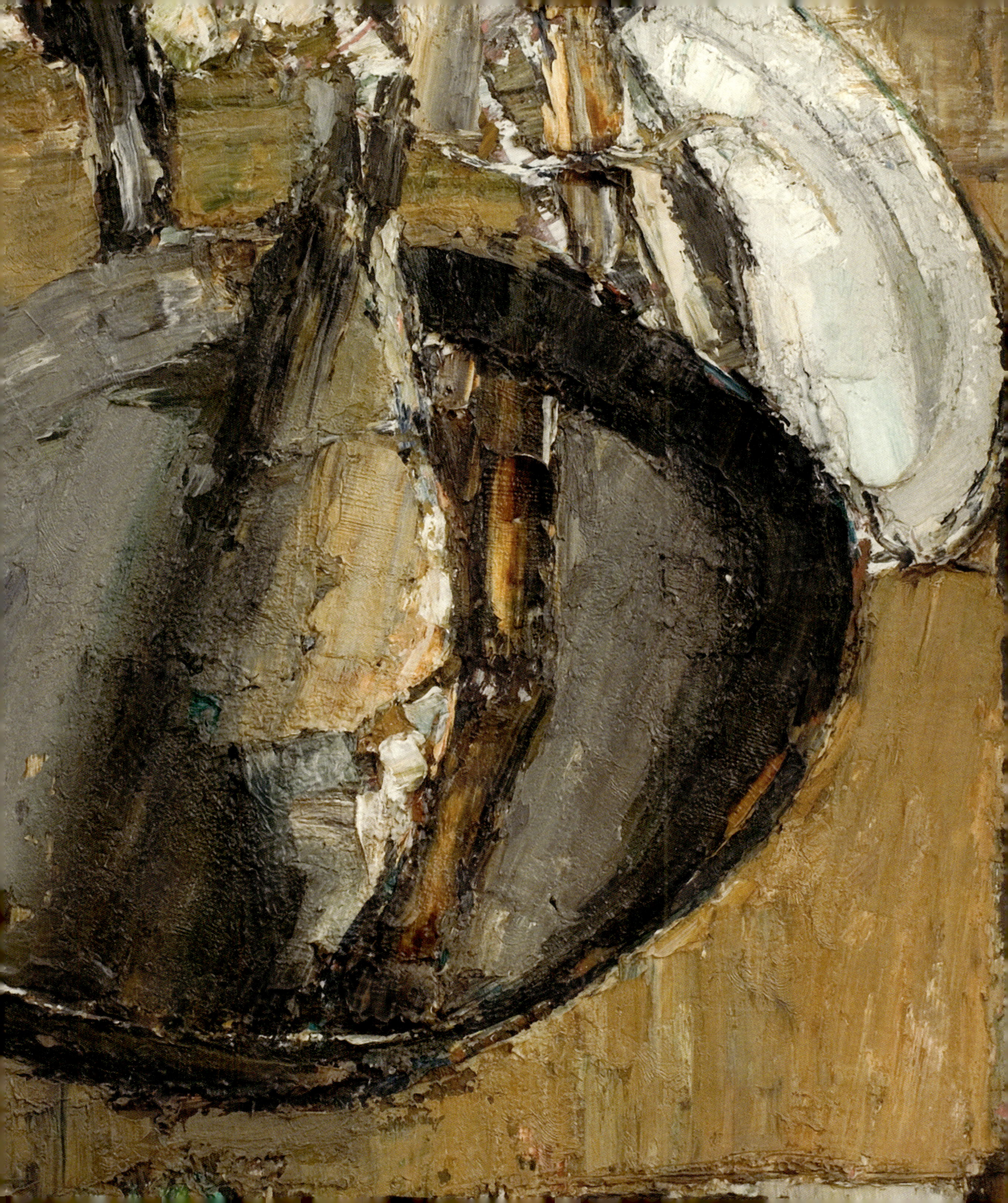

6

Tree I, c.1957

Signed lower right 'Peter Coker'
Inscribed on reverse 'COKER 18 AUG'
Charcoal and conté on paper
54.7 × 74.3 cm | 21½ × 29¼ in

Provenance
Zwemmer Gallery (label on reverse)
Mrs J Lloyd, 26 November 1959 (label on reverse)
Private Collection, UK

Exhibitions
1959, Zwemmer Gallery, *Peter Coker*, no. 15.

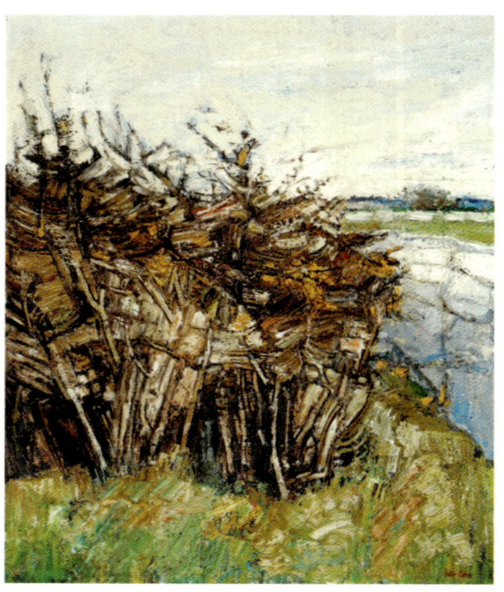

Fig. 3, Peter Coker, *The Gorse Bush*, 1957   Tate, London

In Easter 1955, Coker undertook his first trip exploring France beyond Paris, travelling to Barbizon and the Fontainebleau Forest, and Étretat on the Normandy Coast. Both sites were intimately associated with the French Romantic tradition but Coker's trip was an homage to Courbet, who spent prolonged periods of time in Barbizon and Étretat. Each location made an immediate, powerful impression upon Coker, so much so that he returned that summer and the Easter of the following year, expanding his travels to include Audierne, associated with de Staël. Coker's drawings and subsequent paintings during this first foray into the French landscape formed the basis for his second exhibition at Zwemmer Gallery in 1957. *Tree I* was included in his third show with the Zwemmer Gallery in 1959, but stylistically relates to the era of *Gorse Bush*, 1957 [Fig. 3], Tate, the product of a summer 1957 trip to Étretat and Audierne, Coker's first driving expedition abroad upon passing his driving test.

In *Tree I*, a single tree fills the sheet of paper with a wall or hedge behind. Alongside forest scenes, both in France and at home, Coker frequently depicted lone trees, not necessarily magnificent ancient boughs but trees that 'confronted' him. John Russell Taylor described Coker's search for the tree that could inspire: "like Monet on his first trip to the Riviera, he realized that just any tree would not do it, it had to be the right tree, and he would know it only when he saw it."[17] This tree literally and metaphorically dominates the work, assuming an anthropomorphically human presence.

The drawing is heavily worked in charcoal and conté, Coker's usual drawing materials: "I probably over-densify things anyway, no doubt because of the physical nature of the work, the pressure, possibly because of the speed and directness of statement that I want."[18] The density of mark-making in *Tree I* augments the packed composition, reflecting the sensation of compactness Coker experienced in the environs of Audierne. In a letter Coker addressed to the Tate upon presenting *Gorse Bush* to the gallery in 1986 in memory of his son, Coker wrote, "I moved to the coast, making notes and drawings of the lighthouse, the sea, coastal fields, stonewalls, cabbage plots and close-ups of gorse and bracken bushes. Everything happened at eye level, the fields were separated from the shore by stone walls some four feet above the water line."[19]

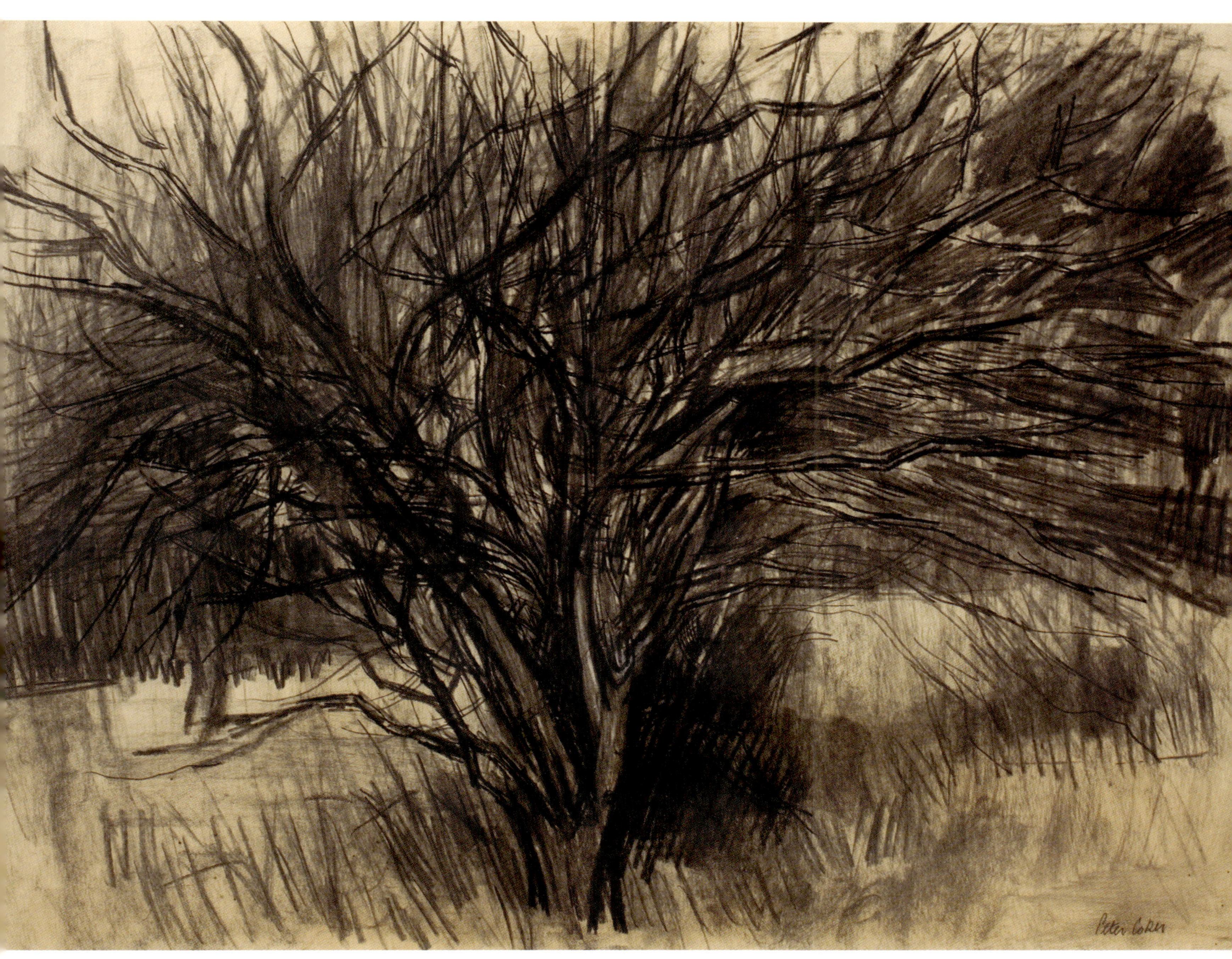

Sunflowers, 1958-59

Signed lower right 'Peter Coker'
Oil on hardboard
120 × 97 cm | 47^1/$_4$ × 38^1/$_4$ in

Provenance
Kemper Collection
Private Collection, UK

Literature
David Wootton with contributions by John Russell
Taylor and Richard Humphreys, *Peter Coker RA*
(Chris Beetles Ltd, 2002), cat. rais. no. 69, p. 120.
A. Lambirth and C. Etter, *A monographic exploration
of Peter Coker's 1958-9 'Sunflowers'* (Piano Nobile
Publications, 2012).

Exhibitions
1959, London, Zwemmer Gallery, *Peter Coker*, no. 3.
2012/13, Madrid, Fundación Juan March, *Treasure
Island: British Art from Holbein to Hockney*,
no. 156, pp. 280-1, col. ill., p. 281.

Sunflowers, 1958-59, is the first of three oil paintings depicting of a bunch of sunflowers that Coker produced between 1958 and 1961, alongside a set of drawings of whole sunflowers and their constituent parts including the charcoal work, *Sunflower Head*, 1958. The second oil, *Sunflowers*, 1960, resides in an international Private Collection whilst the last in the trio, *Sunflowers*, 1961 [Fig. 4], is in the collection of Pallant House Gallery, Chichester. Coker would undoubtedly have appreciated the historical precedent to his motif in Van Gogh's iconic sunflowers but a reason more pragmatic than evocative lay behind the choice of subject. Sunflowers grew in abundance in the garden of Coker's London home but, when Coker and his family moved to Essex, the theme came to a natural halt as sunflowers would not take in the new garden. Still-lifes held an important role in Coker's early works – this was amongst the last subject that could claim to adhere to this genre before landscape took precedence.

Sunflowers is monumental in scale, echoing the statuesque sunflower, though Coker always had a predisposition towards the grandiose, heightening effect through literal aggrandisement. A generous bunch of stems sits in a vase, the yellow heads and rich green of the foliage offset by the umber background, the autumnal colours fitting for the typical blooming of sunflowers in late summer. With heads bowed to the ground, as if in lament for their passing, and beginning to shrivel, the flowers have passed from glorious bloom to melancholy wilt. The symbolism of drooping, dying flowers evidently captured Coker's imagination far more than sunflowers in full splendour. Drawn to the ominous and turbulent in landscapes, even in this joyous abundance of sunflowers, Coker asserts the inescapable synchronicity of the forces of life and death. Laden with thick oil paint applied in broad, unbroken swathes, the surface of *Sunflowers* is overwhelmingly smooth and impenetrable. Texture is homogenous across the painting – lush, almost glossy oil paint draws the viewer to scrutinise the surface. The sheer weight and solidity of the painting states its objecthood. As Coker argued, the "solidity...is all to do with recreating nature and making an equivalently solid object."[20] Paint itself - tangible matter - was the primary protagonist throughout Coker's career.

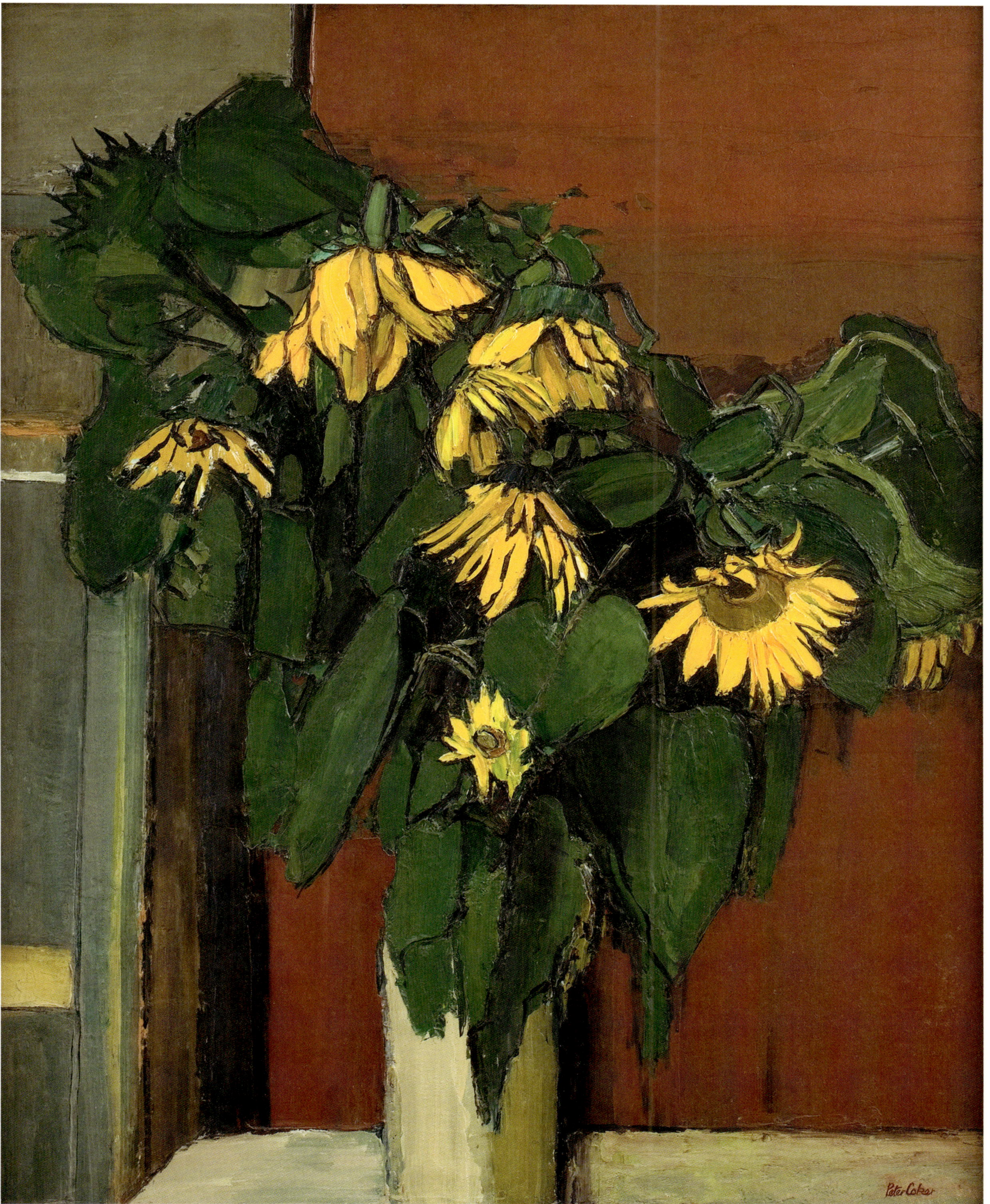

Peter Coker

Sunflower Head, 1958

Titled, signed and dated lower right
'Sunflower Head Peter Coker 1958'
Charcoal on paper
53 × 72 cm | 20⅞ × 28⅞ in

Provenance
Private Collection, UK

Literature
A. Lambirth and C. Etter, *A monographic exploration of Peter Coker's 1958-9 'Sunflowers'* (Piano Nobile Publications, 2012), col ill. p. 6.

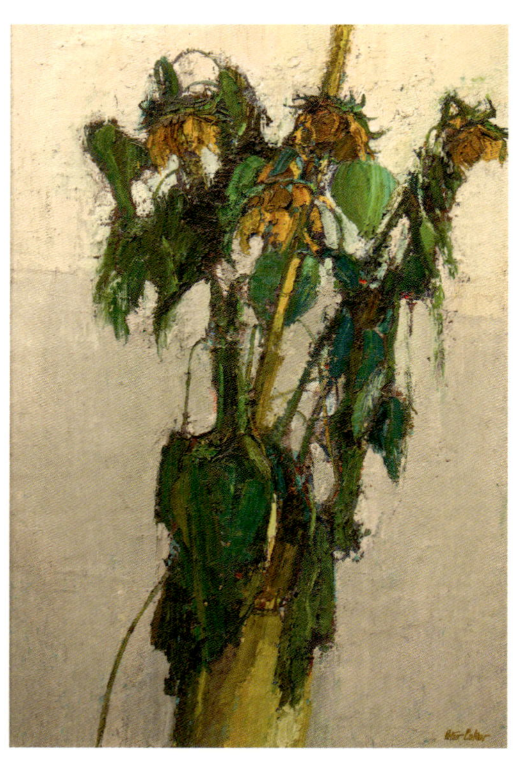

Fig. 4, Peter Coker, *Sunflowers*, 1961   Pallant House Gallery, Bequest of Mrs Vera Coker in memory of Peter Coker (2014)

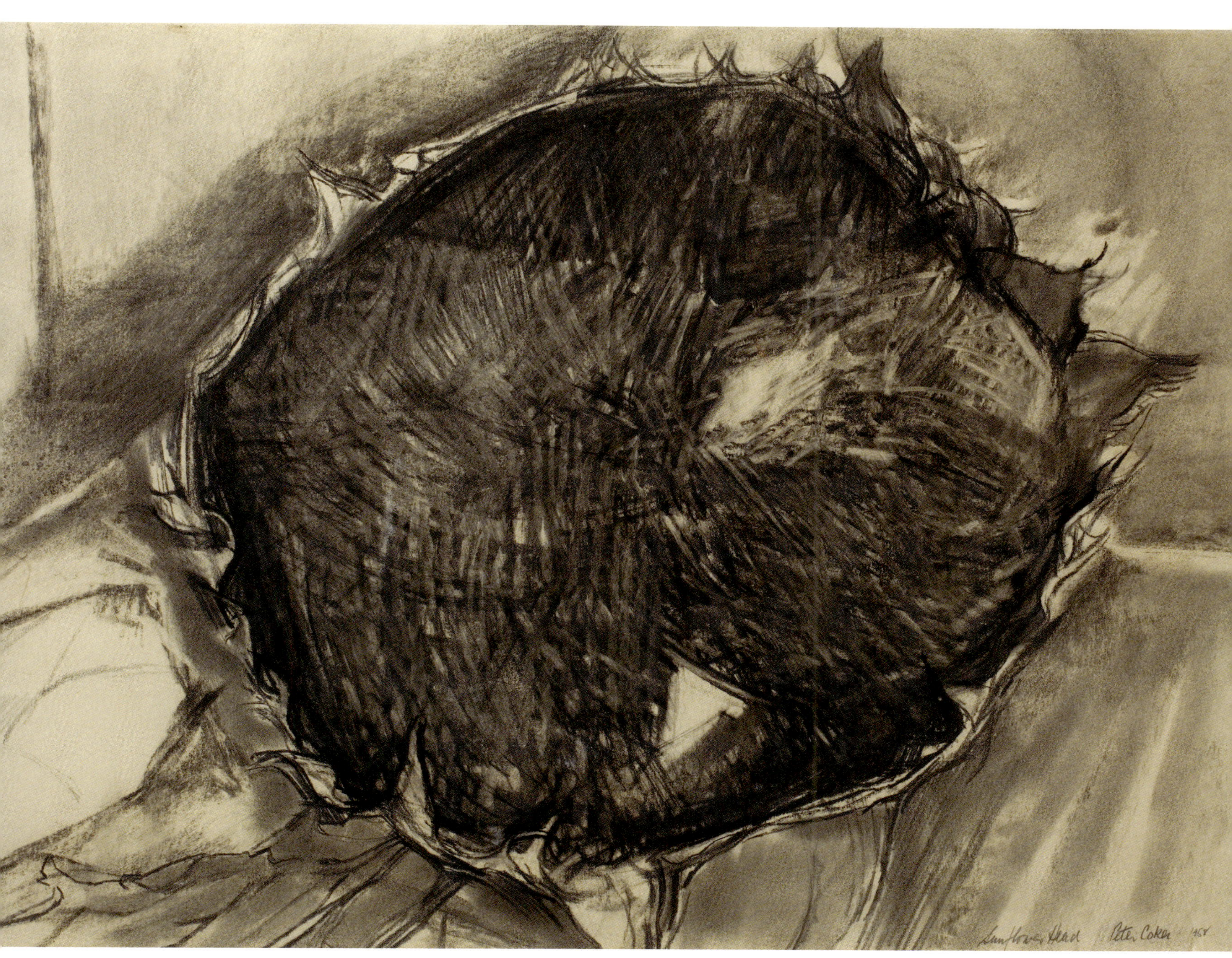
Sunflower Head   Peter Coker   1958

Forest IV, 1959

Signed lower right 'Peter Coker'
Signed and titled on reverse
'Peter Coker Forest IV'
Oil on canvas
123.5 × 81.5 cm | 48⅝ x 32⅛ in

Provenance
Zwemmer Gallery
Dr Gil Park Collection
Private Collection, USA

Literature
David Wootton with contributions by John Russell
Taylor and Richard Humphreys, *Peter Coker RA*
(Chris Beetles Ltd, 2002), cat. rais. no. 75, p. 120,
col. ill. p. 64.

Exhibitions
1959, London, Zwemmer Gallery, *Peter Coker*, no. 9.
1959, Manchester, Tib Lane Gallery, *A Selection of
Young Contemporaries*, no. 21.

In the summer of 1958, Coker undertook a pilgrimage to Antibes in southern France, the town to which de Staël retreated in 1953 and where he ultimately committed suicide in 1955. The trip was resoundingly disappointing and Coker did not return to France until 1965. Instead, for seven years he immersed himself in the ancient forests and coastlines closer to home. Working at Colchester School of Art, Coker befriended the community of artists based in East Anglia including Edward Bawden and John Nash, moving with his family to Mistley on the border between North Essex and Suffolk in 1962. Whilst Bawden and Nash represented a quintessentially British school, rooted in the romantic tradition of bucolic rural scenes, Coker channeled the spirit of de Staël in his woodland landscapes, producing scenes that were familiar and yet startlingly modern.

For Coker's third solo exhibition with Zwemmer Gallery in 1959, Epping Forest served as his artistic muse: he produced nine oils and seven drawings that constituted the heart of the show. *Forest IV* and *Forest VI*, both painted in 1959, were works 9 and 11 in the Zwemmer Gallery catalogue respectively. *Forest VI* is, exceptionally, painted on board – Coker shifted away from the wooden supports of previous works and moved to employing canvases for the Epping Forest series, initiating a trajectory towards canvas as his standard backing. In both works, Coker focuses on the lower regions of the forest – a maze of tree trunks spring from the forest ground, transitioning from singularly defined trees into the background of a haze of greenery.

The presence of de Staël is palpable in both *Forest IV* and *Forest VI*. In an extended passage discussing the tangible influence of de Staël on his work, Coker stated: "De Staël has this wonderful sense of *matière* which especially appealed to me. Also the degree to which he took reality towards abstraction without departing from it. But also the actual physical nature of overlapping and underlaying. The verticality of de Staël was very sympathetic to me. I found myself being constricted by three dimensional depth and wanted to lift things up vertically and place them like a series of playing cards, thus creating the space on a vertical plane."[21] The texture of paint, particularly in the immediate foreground of both paintings, echoes de Staël's handling of paint: in *Forest IV* a lush, expressionistic passage describing the golden earth sweeps across the base of the canvas whilst in *Forest VI* the plaster-like texture of paint fractures to reveal a multitude of built-up paint layers. In both works, trunks and branches strain upwards, surging past the uppermost edge of the composition. Verticality reigns supreme whilst an emphasis on formal structure and a uniform consistency of surface threaten to overwhelm legibility of subject. Coker edges towards abstraction, catching himself just on the verge: "you could paint the feeling, the experience of place without actually registering the factual nature of it, though I never lost a sense of the factual world."[22]

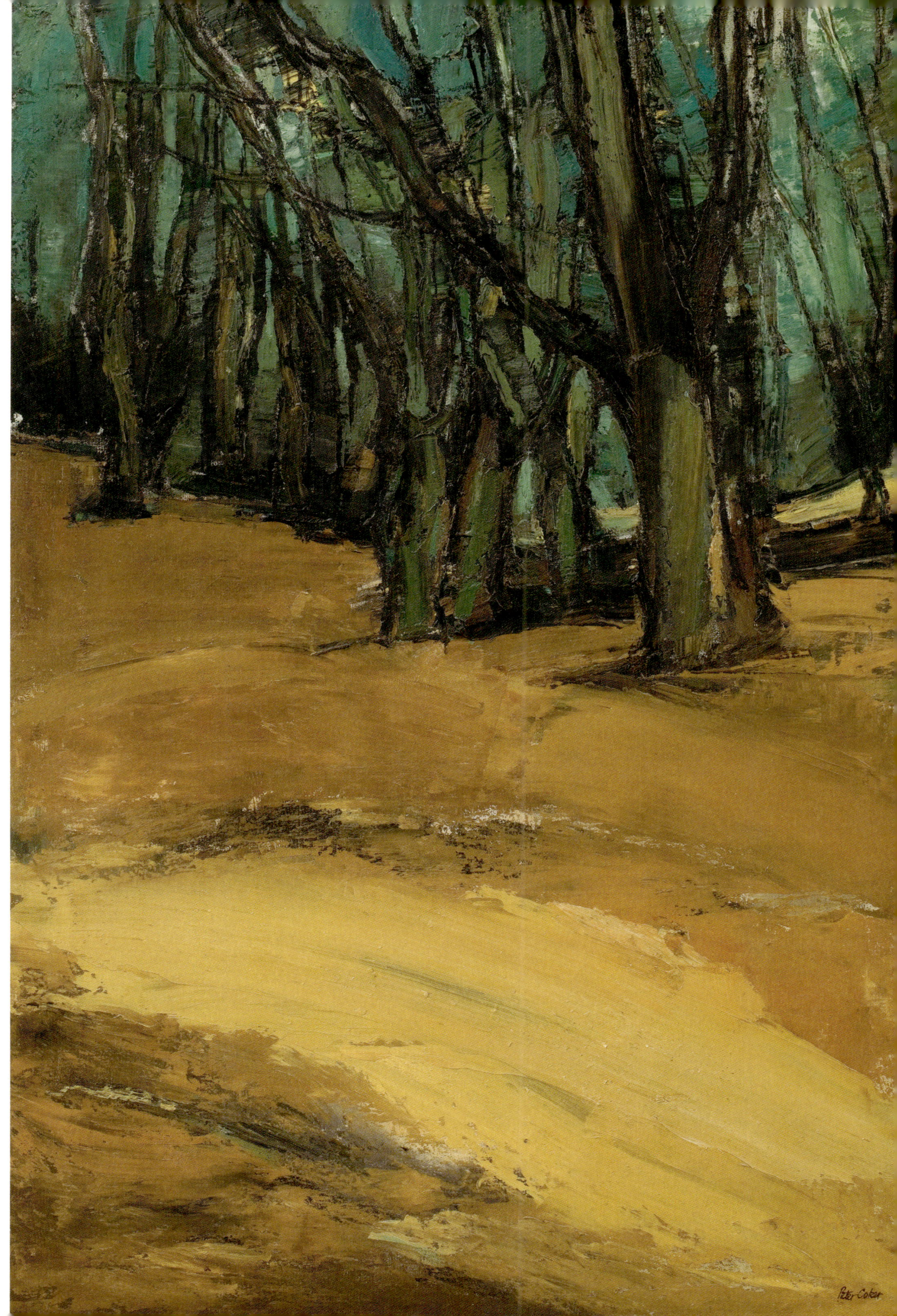

Peter Coker

Forest VI, 1959

Signed lower left 'Peter Coker'
Oil on hardboard
148.6 × 102.2 cm | 58½ × 40¼ in

Provenance
Collection of Lord and Lady Attenborough
Chris Beetles
Private Collection

Literature
David Wootton with contributions by John Russell Taylor
and Richard Humphreys, *Peter Coker RA* (Chris Beetles
Ltd, 2002), cat. rais. no. 77, p. 120, col. ill. p. 65.

Exhibitions
1959, London, Zwemmer Gallery, *Peter Coker*, no. 11.
1972/73, Colchester, The Minories, *Peter Coker RA,
paintings, pastels, drawings, etchings*, no. 21; touring to Bath,
Victoria Gallery; London, The Morley Gallery; Sheffield,
Mappin Art Gallery.
1977, London, Royal Academy of Arts, *British Painting
1952-1977*, no. 77.
1992/93, Kendal, Abbot Hall Art Gallery, *Peter Coker:
Landscapes 1955-1991*, no. 4; a selection of works
transferring to London, Royal Academy of Arts; Carlisle,
Tullie House; Ipswich, Christchurch Mansion.

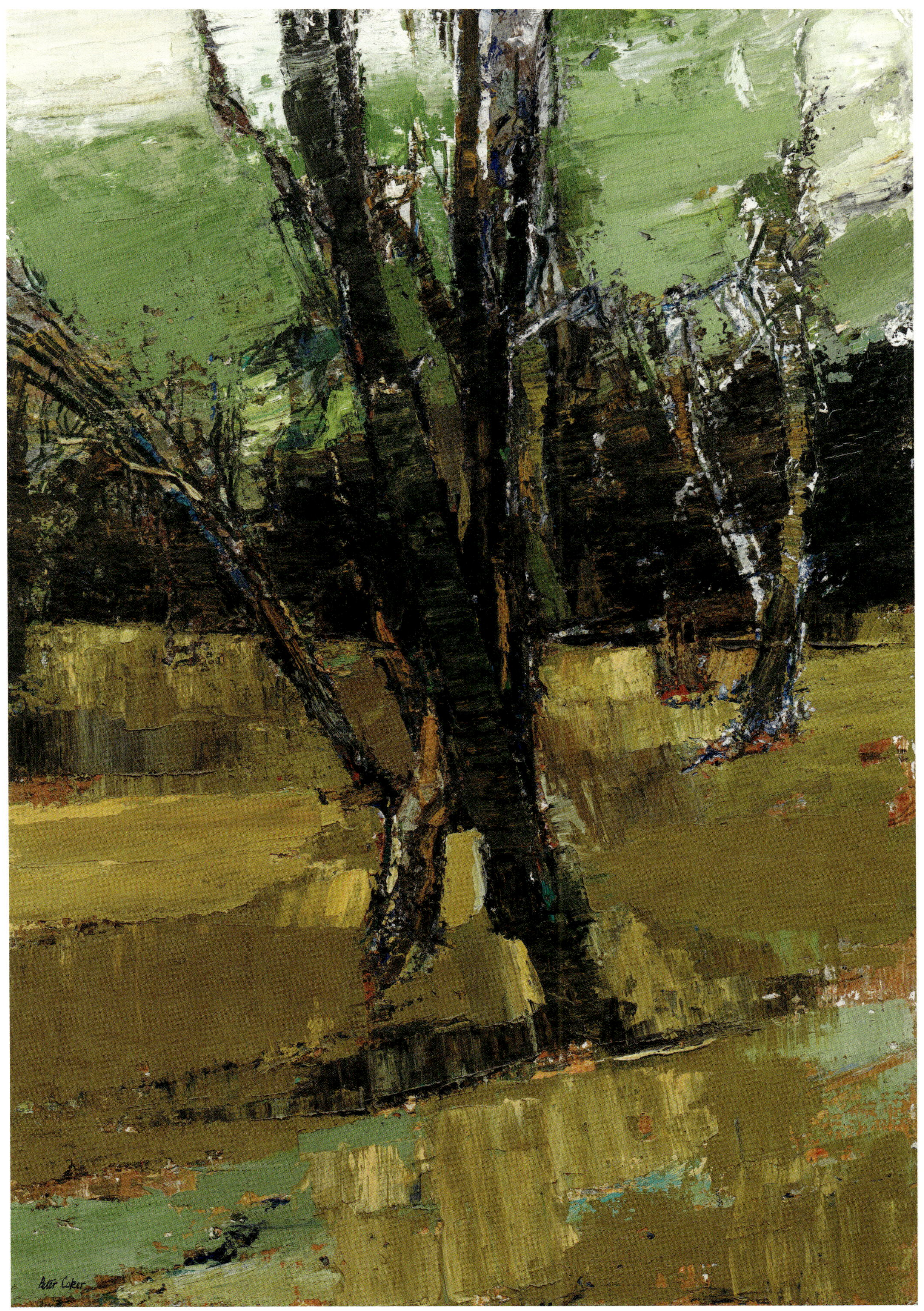
Peter Coker

11

Seascape, 1959

Signed lower left 'Peter Coker'
Oil on millboard
152.4 × 121.9 cm | 60 × 48 in

Provenance
Zwemmer Gallery (label on reverse)
Provost Collection
Private Collection

Literature
David Wootton with contributions by John Russell
Taylor and Richard Humphreys, *Peter Coker RA*
(Chris Beetles Ltd, 2002), cat. rais. no. 81, p. 120.

Exhibitions
1959, London, Zwemmer Gallery, *Peter Coker*, no. 4.
1960, London, Royal Academy of Arts, *Summer
Exhibition*, no. 169.
1965, London, Zwemmer Gallery, *Summer
Exhibition*, no number.
1967, London, Zwemmer Gallery, *Peter Coker,
An exhibition of paintings and drawings*, no. 9.
1972/73, Colchester, The Minories, *Peter Coker RA,
paintings, pastels, drawings, etchings*, no. 20; touring
to Bath, Victoria Gallery; London, The Morley
Gallery; Sheffield, Mappin Art Gallery.

Various influences fuse in *Seascape*, transfigured by Coker's singular vision into a
scene of guttural rawness. Depicting a churning sea off the Étretat shore, it is not
just the spectre of Courbet lingering in Étretat as a location but his specific paintings
of turbulent seascapes, such as *The Stormy Sea*, 1870; Musée d'Orsay, that Coker
echoes. The vertical orientation, however, is inherited from Nicolas de Staël as is the
application of paint. The overcast sky, built up in a loose patchwork of dry, scraped-
over greens and purples, echoes the interlocking blocks of paint that constitute skies
in de Staël's landscapes. The agitated sea, ever tossing, is captured by Coker with
sculptural solidity: effervescent white horses are built up over time in layers of white
impasto paint. The watery turmoil is reflected in the heavily-worked paint – any
method of smearing, layering, dragging, scratching, moulding, scumbling paint goes.
The immense force of crashing waves is given the full weight of Coker's loaded palette
knife.

Frederick Gore has suggested that, alongside de Staël, Jackson Pollock – in a general
rather than specific sense – lay behind the freedom and bravura with which Coker
worked his materials: "Pollock also suggested to many European figurative painters
that the accidents of paint could stand for the uncontrolled or unaccountable aspects
of nature and the natural action of the painter's arm could be a symbol for the
movements of nature."[23] Although European in spirit and decidedly independent in
approach, Coker's work is nonetheless undoubtedly situated within the zeitgeist of
post-war British figurative painting that embraced materiality and extolled arduous and
convoluted process.

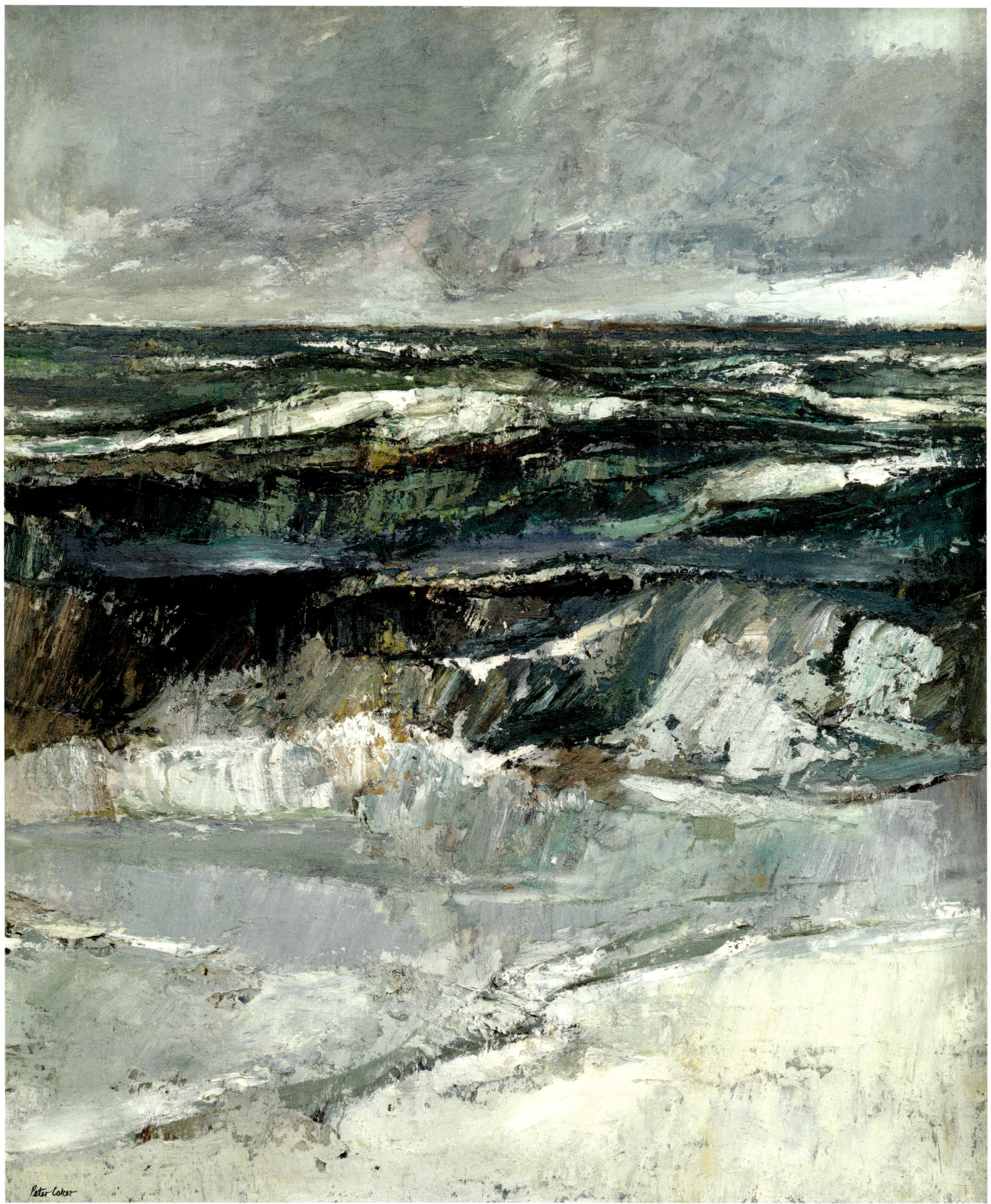
Peter Coker

12

Aldeburgh I, 1964

Signed lower right 'Peter Coker'
Inscribed and dated 'High Sea,
Aldeburgh, Suffolk April 1964'
Oil on board
121.9 × 121.9 cm | 48 × 48 in

Provenance
Collection of the artist
Piano Nobile (label on reverse)
Private Collection, UK

Literature
David Wootton with contributions by John Russell Taylor and
Richard Humphreys, *Peter Coker RA*
(Chris Beetles Ltd, 2002), cat. rais. no. 101, p. 121, col. ill. p. 69.

Exhibitions
1964, London, Zwemmer Gallery, *Peter Coker*, no. 17.
1965, London, Royal Academy of Arts, *Summer Exhibition*, no. 156.
1972/73, Colchester, The Minories, *Peter Coker RA,*
paintings, pastels, drawings, etchings, no. 26,
as *Aldeburgh*; touring to Bath, Victoria Gallery; London,
The Morley Gallery; Sheffield, Mappin Art Gallery.
1978, Chelmsford, Chelmsford and Essex Museum,
Works by Peter Coker R.A., no. 15.
2005, London, Piano Nobile, *Peter Coker*, no number,
col. ill., p. 9 and front cover.

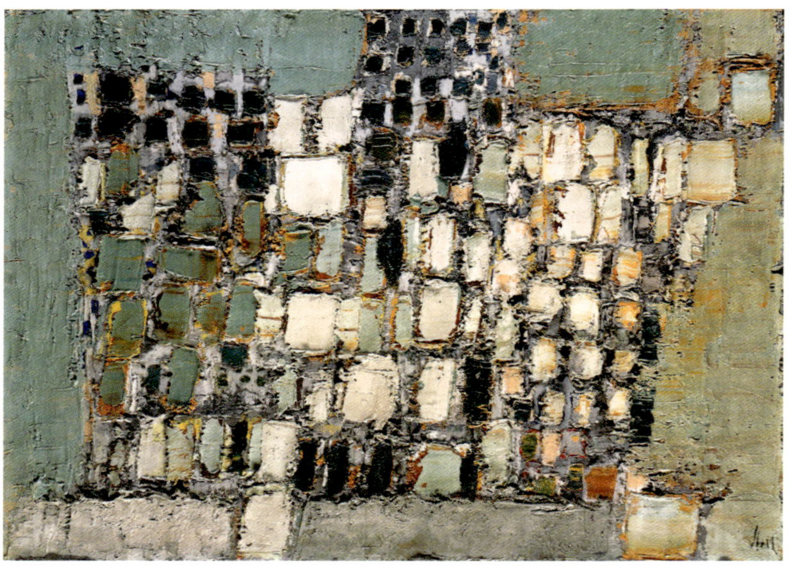
Fig. 5, Nicolas de Staël (1914 – 1955) *Composition 1951*, 1951   Private Collection

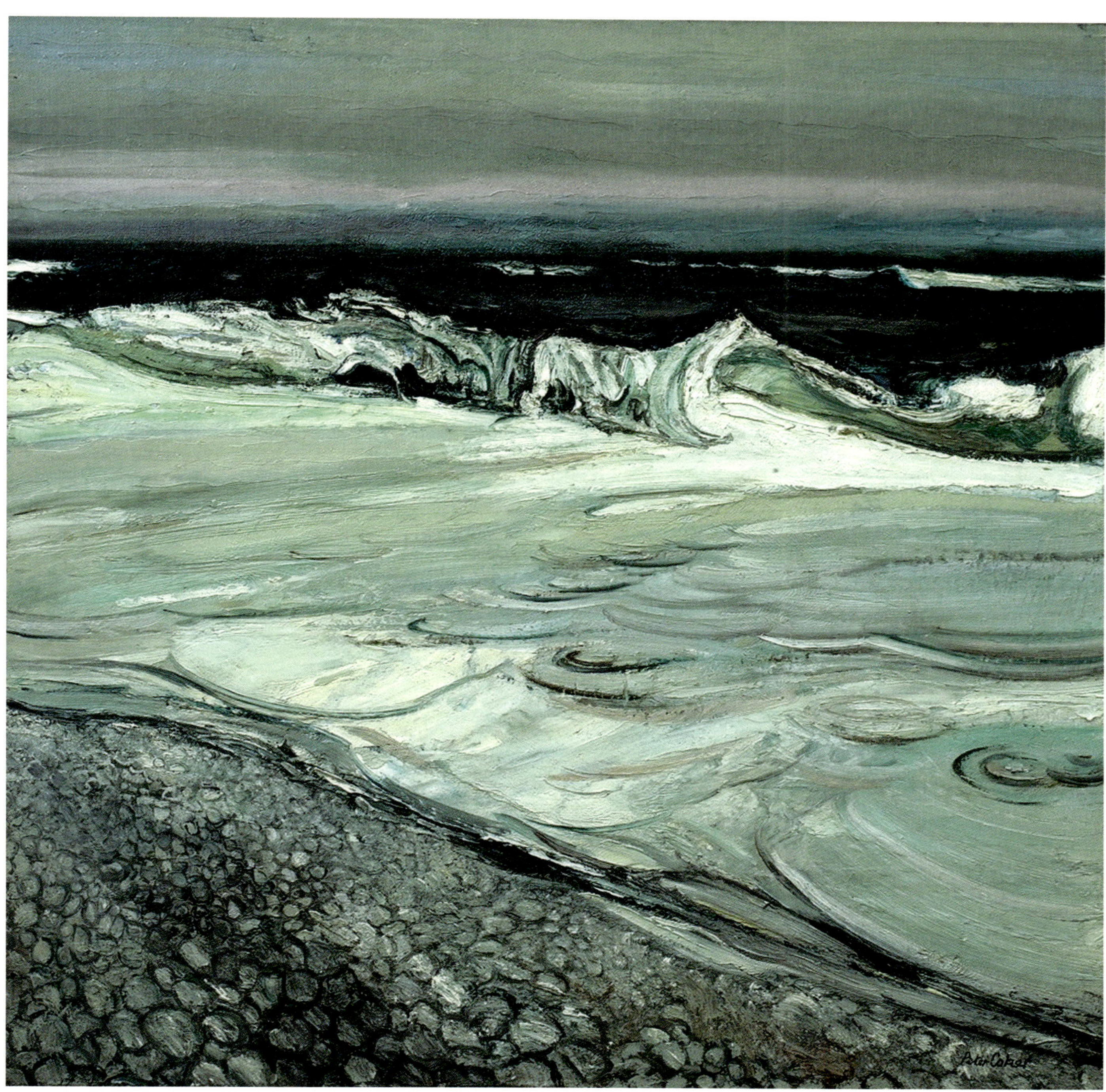

Aldeburgh, on the North Sea coast in Suffolk, represented the northernmost point of East Anglia that Coker ventured to whilst mining the region for atmospheric vistas. Returning frequently to Aldeburgh, Coker rented a flat on the first floor of Tower House, then owned by Bruce Killeen, a colleague of Coker's at Colchester School of Art. From the windows of Tower House, Coker could survey the broad expanse of sea lapping the shingle shoreline. Speaking in 1989, Coker described the act of painting as a "confrontation" with nature – an element of struggle, of menace or peril punctuates his early landscapes.[24] Avidly avoiding the nostalgia of the 'picturesque', Coker instead produces works like *Aldeburgh I*, 1964, that overwhelm with visceral immediacy. Staring down a tempestuous sea face-on, the viewer is engulfed by nature as the surging waves of high tide must be swirling around his or her proverbial feet.

Acutely aware of the weight of tradition and immersed in the legacies of the artists he held in esteem, *Aldeburgh I* is an assured synthesis of artistic references that inform Coker's distinctive sensibility. Whilst the precedent of Courbet's stormy seas holds strong as with *Seascape* [cat. 11], the pink hues of a setting sun over a turbulent North Sea inescapably recalls the British tradition of threatening seascapes, particularly those of JMW Turner. The narrow band of sky visible above a high horizon line echoes a motif found in de Staël's horizons, that of building up strata of colour as seen in works such as *Fontenay*, 1952; Private Collection. The view of Aldeburgh beach is slightly angled down the shore so the waves break on the horizontal and a triangle of shingle is visible in the lower left of the composition. Coker's delineation of individual pebbles instantly recalls works such as de Staël's *Composition 1951*, 1951; Private Collection [Fig. 5], with its idiosyncratic accumulation of askew rectangular blocks of paint.

Comparing *Aldeburgh I* with the earlier *Seascape*, Coker substitutes towering waves more akin to rock faces than water with whirling white foam. High tide waves crash up the shore, eddying and swirling in foaming pools before being subsumed into the next wave, which – in *Aldeburgh I* – is coiled ready to unleash with full force. The sheath of frothing white encompasses a multiplicity of tones: greens, blues, pinks, greys, even touches of black bleed into one another in marbled vortices. Ever conscious of his artistic forefathers, Coker wore the inheritance he assumed lightly, producing in *Aldeburgh I* a work that reverberates with historical echoes and yet is entirely original and ferociously modern.

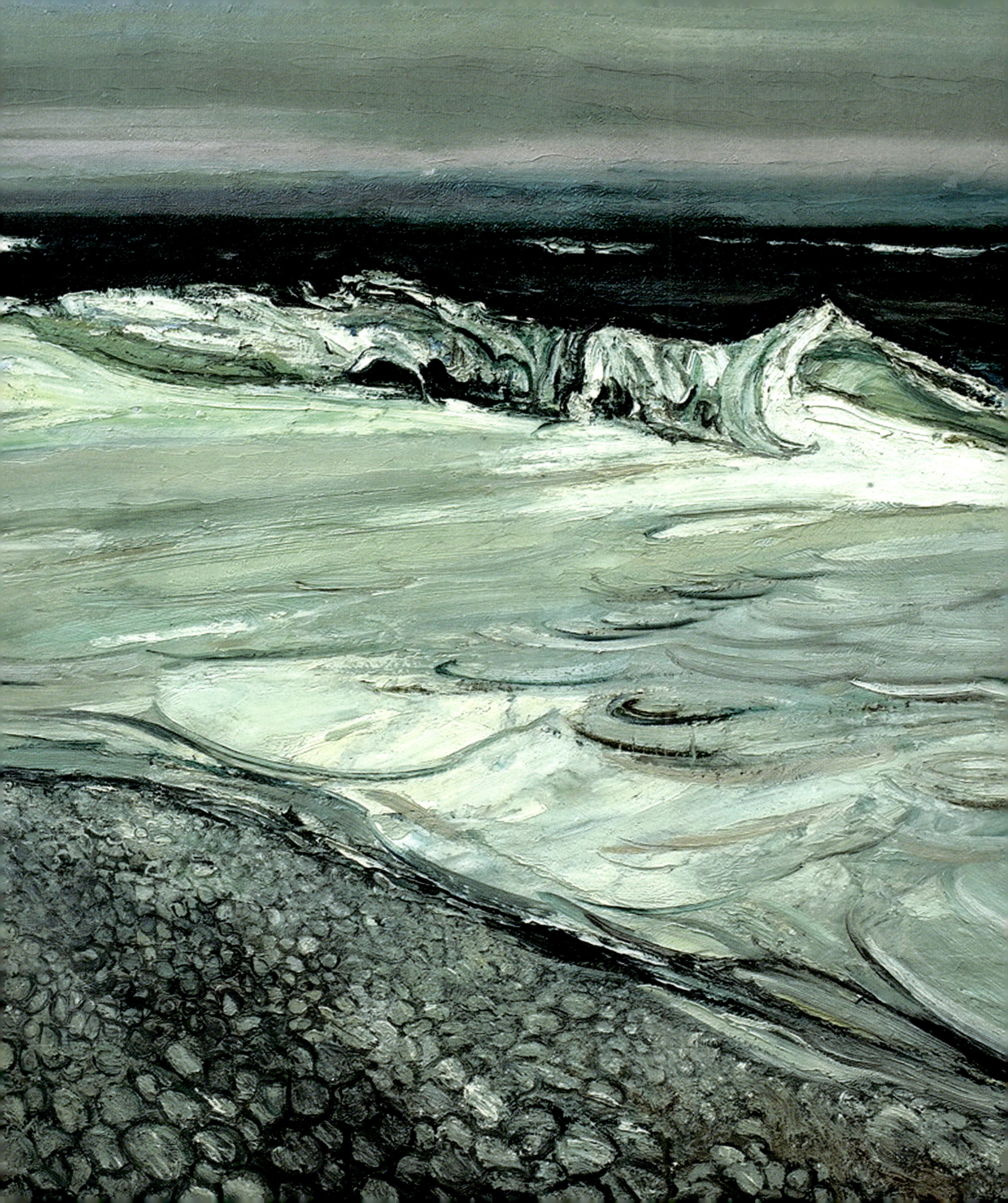

Tunstall Forest I, 1964

Signed lower right 'Peter Coker'
Signed and inscribed with title and
date on reverse 'June 1964 "Tunstall Forest"
Peter Coker'
Oil on canvas
86.4 × 111.8 cm | 34 × 44 in

Provenance
Chris Beetles Gallery
Private Collection, UK

Literature
David Wootton with contributions by John Russell
Taylor and Richard Humphreys, *Peter Coker RA*
(Chris Beetles Ltd, 2002), cat. rais. no. 113, p. 121, col.
ill. p. 68.

Exhibitions
1964, London, Zwemmer Gallery, *Peter Coker*, no. 21.
1979, London, Fieldborne Gallery, *City and Guilds
of London Art School, One Hundred Years*, no. 55.

The woodlands of East Anglia continued to be a source of inspiration for Coker into the 1960s following the first group of Epping Forest works he produced in 1959. In Suffolk, Coker frequented Rendlesham Forest and Tunstall Forest: the latter was the subject of *Tunstall Forest I* and *Tunstall Forest*, painted in June and July of 1964 respectively. That same year, Coker had an exhibition at Zwemmer Gallery almost exclusively devoted to works of woods and individual trees – *Tunstall Forest I* was work 21 in the show.

Whilst *Tunstall Forest* harked back to the Epping Forest works of the 1959 Zwemmer Gallery show with its vertical orientation and accumulated layers of worked impasto paint, *Tunstall Forest I* illustrated an evolution in Coker's practice. Looking across a horizontal sweep of the landscape, *Tunstall Forest I* has a certain lyricism previously unexplored in Coker's work. Homogenous directional brushwork is suggestive of movement, of rippling grass and swaying boughs. The low viewpoint, almost a worm's eye view as if the viewer were lying in the undergrowth, persists from Coker's earliest landscapes but the expansiveness of the vista is near unprecedented. A broad grassy avenue winds into the heart of the picture, leading the viewer between two flanks of a forest. This potent directional pull is a compositional technique inherited from de Staël. Often seen in de Staël's depictions of harbour jetties, receding so starkly they read as pure geometrical construction, Coker employed this device as early as *Lighthouse, Audierne*, 1957. In *Tunstall Forest I*, the grassy approach acts as a conspiratorial invitation, drawing the eye into the shadows cast by the ancient woodland. A wood of two halves, the left section glows in sunlight whilst the right rests in the gloom of the shadows cast over it by the left elevation, suggesting the raking light of late afternoon. Above, a triangle of clouded sky echoes the receding grassy verge below. Frederick Laws, critic for the *Guardian*, commented in his review of the 1964 Zwemmer exhibition that Coker, "allows [trees] to be, dramatic, elegiac, pure pattern or simple botany."[25] *Tunstall Forest I* and *Tunstall Forest* are the embodiment of this observation: expressive expanses and intimate groves both have their place in Coker's manifold renderings of woodlands.

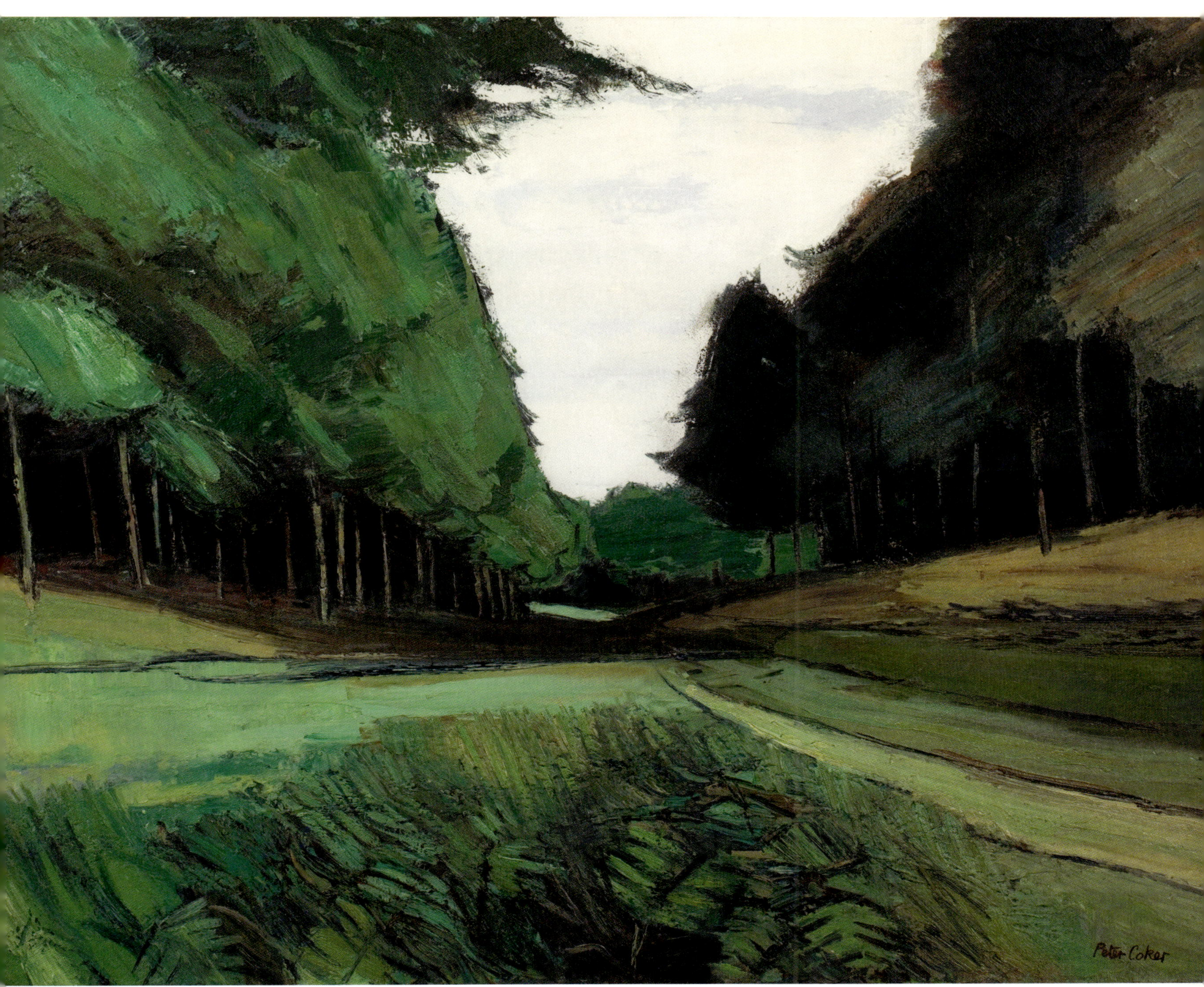
Peter Coker

Tunstall Forest, 1964

Signed lower right 'Peter Coker'
Inscribed with title and dated
'July 1964' on reverse
Oil on canvas
121.3 × 81.3 cm | 47¾ × 32 in

Provenance
Piano Nobile
Private Collection, UK

Literature
David Wootton with contributions by John Russell
Taylor and Richard Humphreys, *Peter Coker RA*
(Chris Beetles Ltd, 2002), cat. rais. no. 116, p. 121.

Exhibitions
1967, London, Royal Academy of Arts,
Summer Exhibition, no. 573.
2005, London, Piano Nobile, *Peter Coker RA*
(1926-2004), p. 6, col. ill. p. 7.

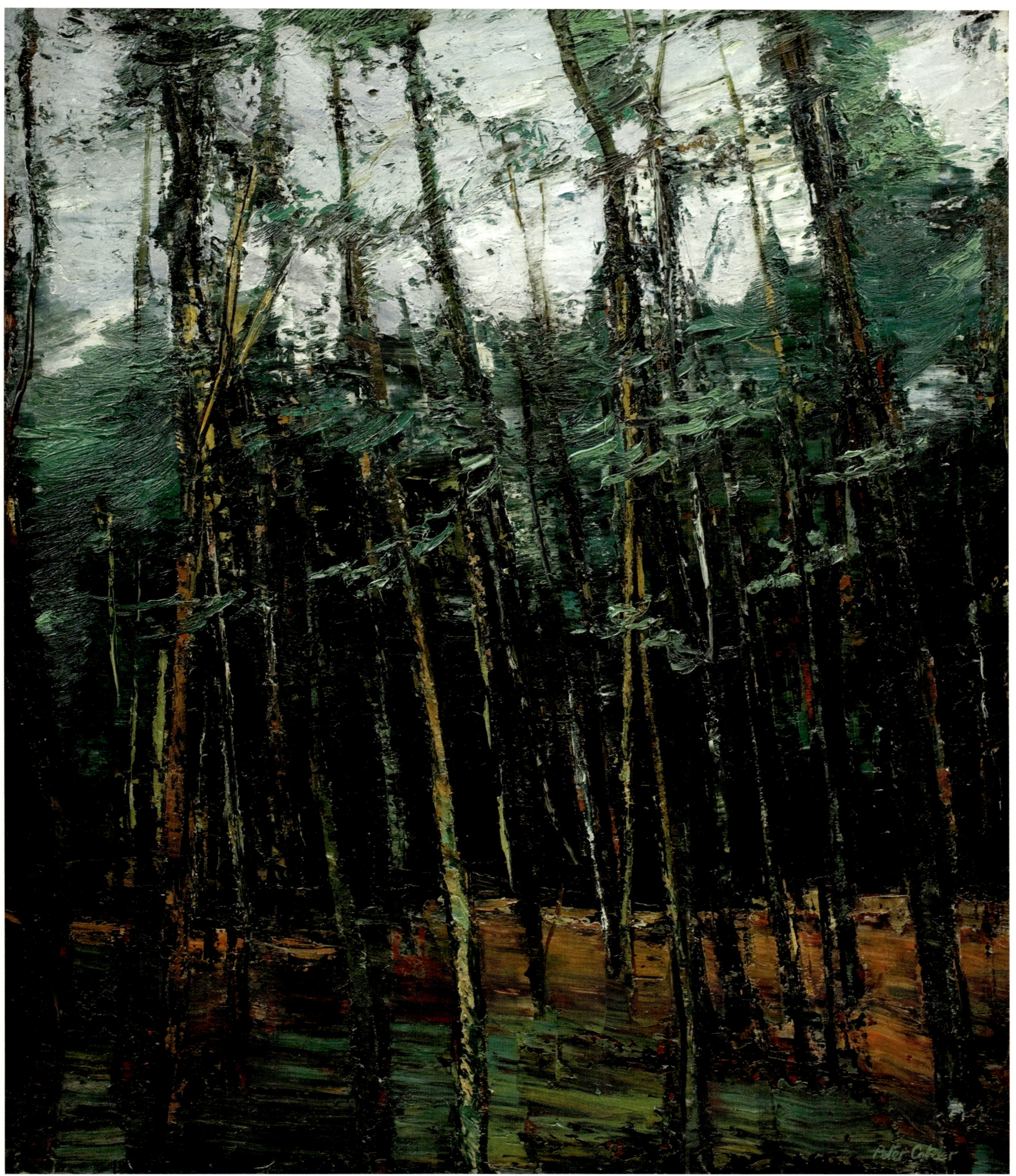
Peter Coker

15

Le Manneport, Étretat, c.1976-7

Signed in pencil lower right 'Peter Coker'
Watercolour on paper laid on card
25.9 × 34.5 cm | 10¼ × 13⅝ in

Provenance
Private Collection, UK

In 1965, Coker returned to France after seven years focusing on the East Anglian landscape. Those sites that had previously proved stimulating acted with magnetic force on Coker, pulling him back. Le Manneport, a rock formation in Étretat – Coker's very first love – was an image that enthralled Coker, as it had previously Claude Monet. Coker produced numerous depictions of Le Manneport in oil, drypoint etching and watercolour as with this iteration.

Le Manneport, Étretat is a watercolour from one of Coker's sketchbooks, extending across a double-page spread and laid onto card. Coker employed sketchbooks whilst working in situ throughout his career but with particular prevalence from the 1970s onwards. These sketchbooks were designed by the artist to include his preferred paper and to be unbound to produce individual works like *Le Manneport, Étretat*, which would most likely have been painted whilst Coker was surveying the coastal scene. An anecdote from Coker's first trip to Étretat in 1955 illustrated the perils of seeking out vantage points that provided stimulating proximity: "On the first full day, he set out to draw under the cliffs, with paper clipped to a piece of hardboard. But, eager to confront the elements directly, he failed to notice the sign that warned against falling rock. A little later, he was surprised when the elements confronted *him*, a piece of rock only just missing him and splitting both drawing [Fig. 6] and board." [26]

Looking down at Le Manneport from a height, the arch of rock is entirely surrounded by the sparkling azure sea, and sky and water are indistinguishable – a bleeding across a near unintelligible horizon line that is often to be seen in de Staël's seascapes. A certain distortion of perspective is in evidence in *Le Manneport, Étretat*, a sensation engendered by the high viewpoint that Coker unashamedly augments: "One of the most important things about de Staël was the flattening of space. Consequently you could paint the feeling, the experience of the place". [27] In stark contrast to his works of the 1950s, *Le Manneport, Étretat* is potently evocative of a gloriously sunny summer's day. The dappled effects of light and shadow, and their reflection off the water, play across the white cliff face. The brilliant palette of gleaming white and jewel-like blue belies an entirely new, and somewhat unexpected, development in Coker's career – the inauguration of the Mediterranean into the roll-call of preferred locations.

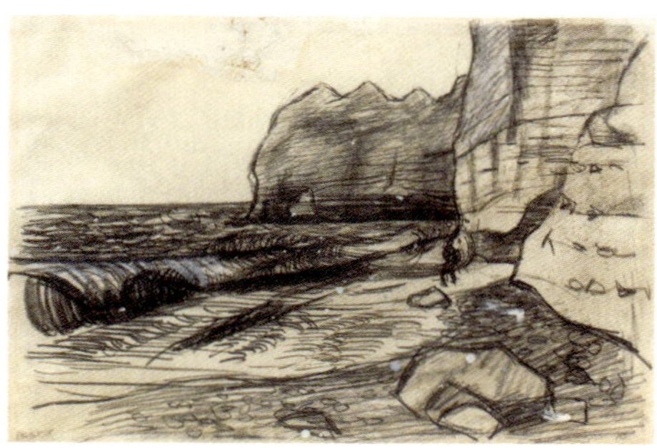

Fig. 6. Peter Coker, *Étretat*, 1955 Piano Nobile

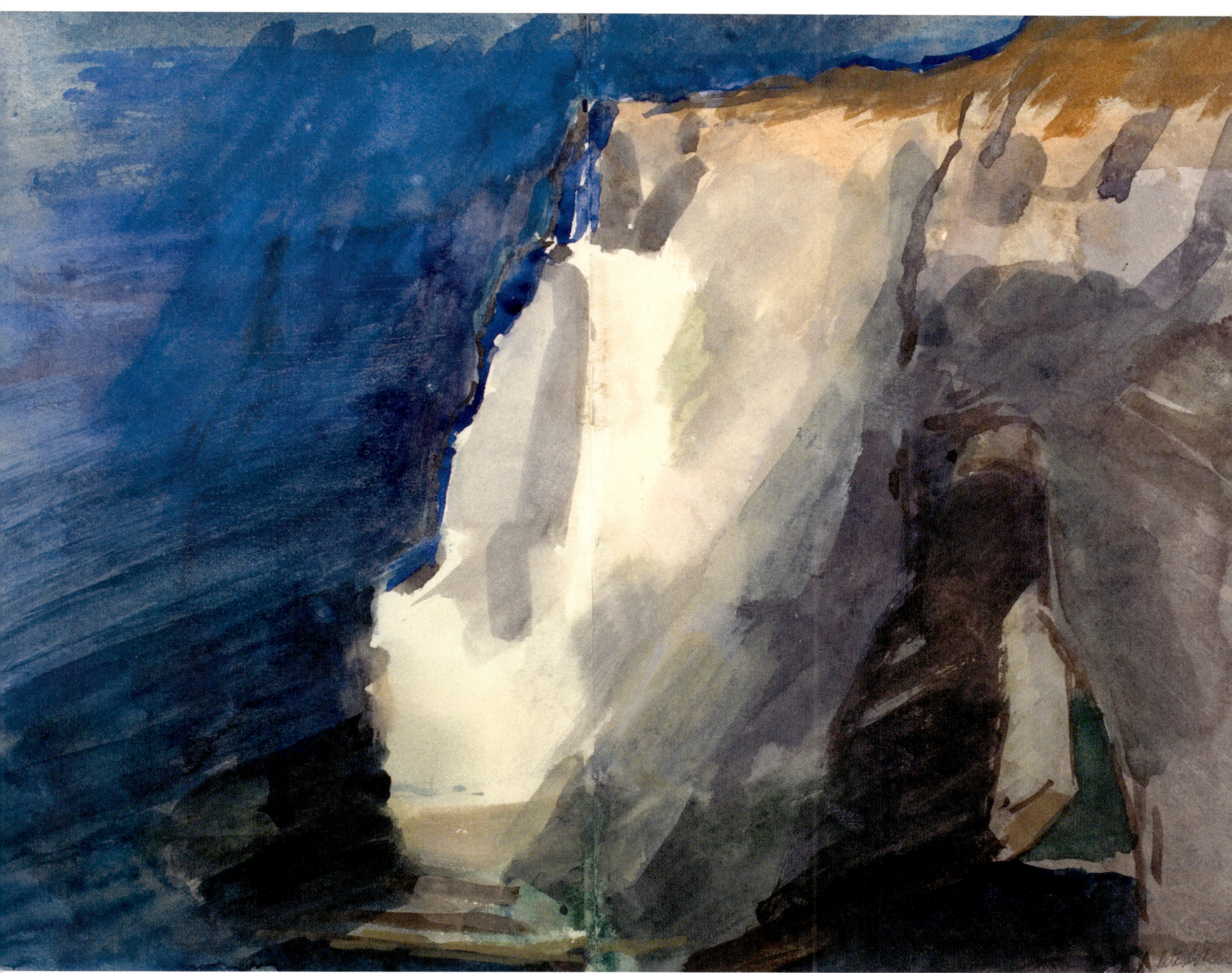

16

Bargemon 2, c.1978

Signed lower left 'Peter Coker'
Oil on canvas
61.5 × 75.7 cm | 24¼ × 29¾ in

Provenance
Miss Marjorie Walpole
Private Collection, UK

Literature
David Wootton with contributions by John Russell
Taylor and Richard Humphreys, *Peter Coker RA*
(Chris Beetles Ltd, 2002), cat. rais. no. 346, p. 130,
col. ill., p. 130.

Exhibitions
1978, London, Thackeray Gallery, *Peter Coker*, no. 9.

In 1958, Coker embarked upon a fruitless expedition to southern France, Antibes
in particular. Instinctively drawn to the northern light and landscape that he knew
intimately, Coker shied away from the exotic unknown of the Mediterranean. By the
1970s, however, the Mediterranean became a location to inspire rather than repulse. By
1975, Coker had established a reliable base in the Medieval hillside town of Bargemon
in the Var, a few miles inland from the Côte d'Azur. His Bargemon residence was
at the invitation of Elsbeth Juda, a friend he met through Roger de Grey, Principal
of the City and Guilds of London School of Art where Coker began teaching in
1974. Picasso, Matisse, Bonnard, and de Staël all lived out the later stages of their
careers in southern France and Coker sought out the many examples of their work
scattered across museums in the region. Grappling with an entirely new environment,
it was unsurprising that Coker looked to his predecessors to scrutinise how the
Mediterranean fared at their accomplished hands. Bargemon become a base from
which Coker explored, captivating works of art and locations alike.

Coker depicts the town in *Bargemon 2* in its quintessential beauty, situated on a low
hill and nestled below higher peaks with church tower rising from the ochre and cream
roofs. The curving path from which the viewer surveys Bargemon envelops the gentle
summit and the surrounding greenery – perhaps woodland. An atmosphere of hazy
warmth pervades the vista, a dusky blurring of colour and form. Even the brushwork
has a certain languid feel of suggestion over precision, of strokes mingling and colours
coalescing on the canvas.

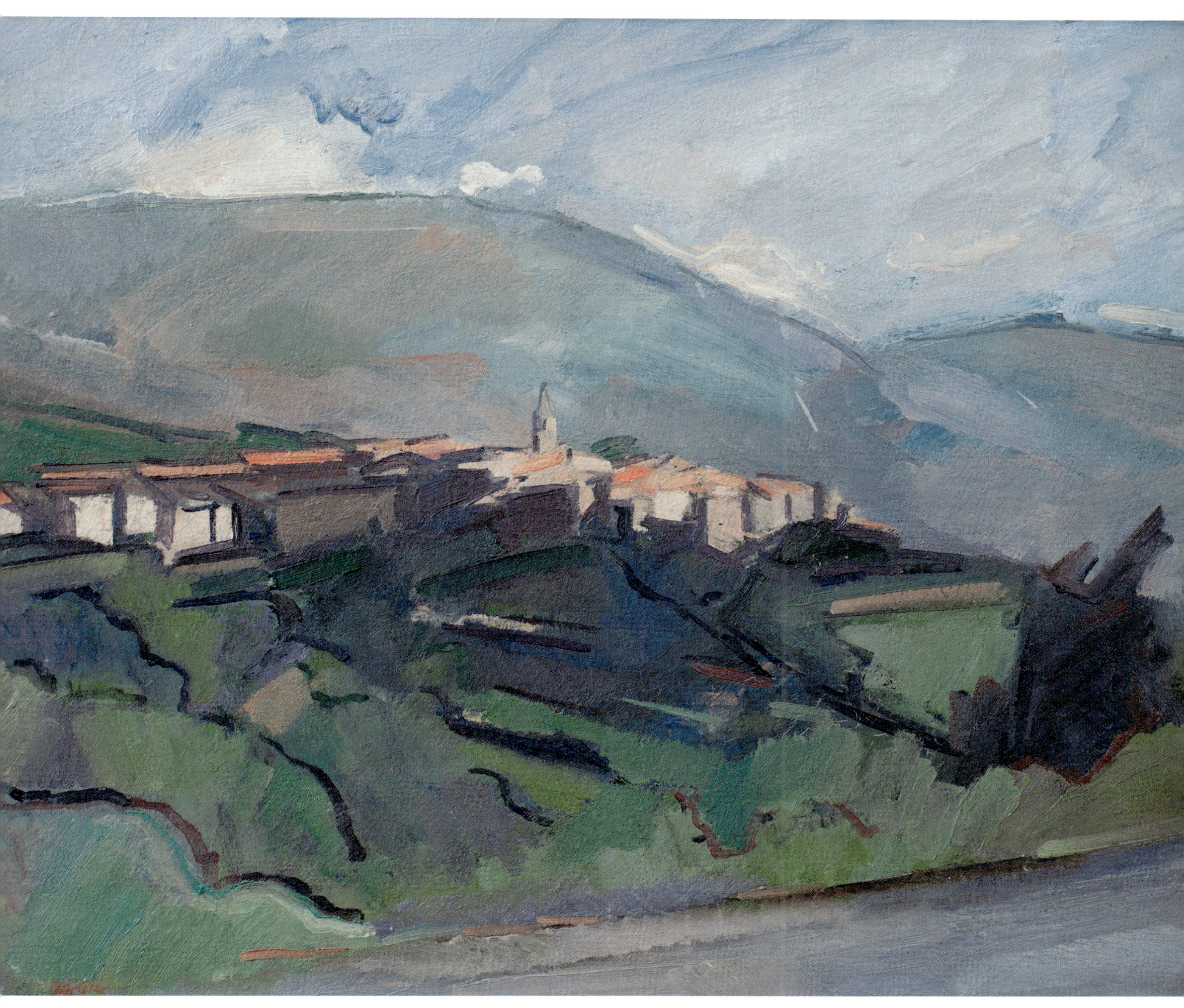

17

The Palm, Château Garden, 1979-80

Signed lower left 'Peter Coker'
Oil on canvas
177.8 × 160 cm | 70 × 63 in

Provenance
G Rodopoulos Collection

Literature
David Wootton with contributions by John Russell
Taylor and Richard Humphreys, *Peter Coker RA*
(Chris Beetles Ltd, 2002), cat. rais. no. 396, p. 133,
col. ill., p. 95.

Exhibitions
1980, London, Gallery 10, *Peter Coker R.A.*, no. 1.

Whilst residing with Elsbeth Juda in Bargemon, Coker was permitted by her friend and neighbour, Elisabeth Collins, to work in the extensive gardens of her home, Le Vieux Château. The exotic and plentiful flora impressed themselves on Coker's imagination and precipitated a number of depictions of bountiful palms and spiky agaves.

In this view, *The Palm, Château Garden*, Coker looks down from a balcony onto a chamaerops palm with an oblique view of railings to the lower left of the composition and the azure blue of a swimming pool to the upper right. The dialogue between interior and exterior – the potential of the threshold and the shifting fall of light – featured prominently in Coker's oeuvre at this juncture in his career. Certainly, *The Palm, Château Garden* bears elements of this perceptual investigation as the natural and the man-made intersect with the wilderness bursting up from the confines of the courtyard. This distinctive angle was the subject of four watercolours and drawings and two canvases including *The Palm, Château Garden*: the other iteration is most likely destroyed. Dramatic or distorted perspectives featured in Coker's work from his earliest Butcher's Shop pieces but this viewpoint is extreme as to verge on the abstract without an explanation of the set-up. Instead, an explosion of furious slashes of yellow, green and black – the preponderance of palm leaves – burgeon from the centre of the picture in a whirl of dynamism. Introducing Coker's 1992 Abbot Hall exhibition, Frederick Gore argued that, "his visual and conceptual experience of a landscape which he has seen and drawn is for him abstract in its forms, colour and texture: in effect an abstract painting. It is deliberately wrought because he is a craftsman, but full of exciting accidents: an object in its own right."[28] Truthfulness to appearance is supplanted by truthfulness to experience: through the animated vortex of strokes of jewel-like colours Coker conveys the heat, the light, the verdant lushness of southern France. Painting sensation necessitated "imagination to be able to manipulate the composition and…creative freedom to alter colours."[29] Coker distorts perspective and heightens colour for "directness of statement", simulating the visceral, fleeting impressions that constitute the most evocative of memories.[30]

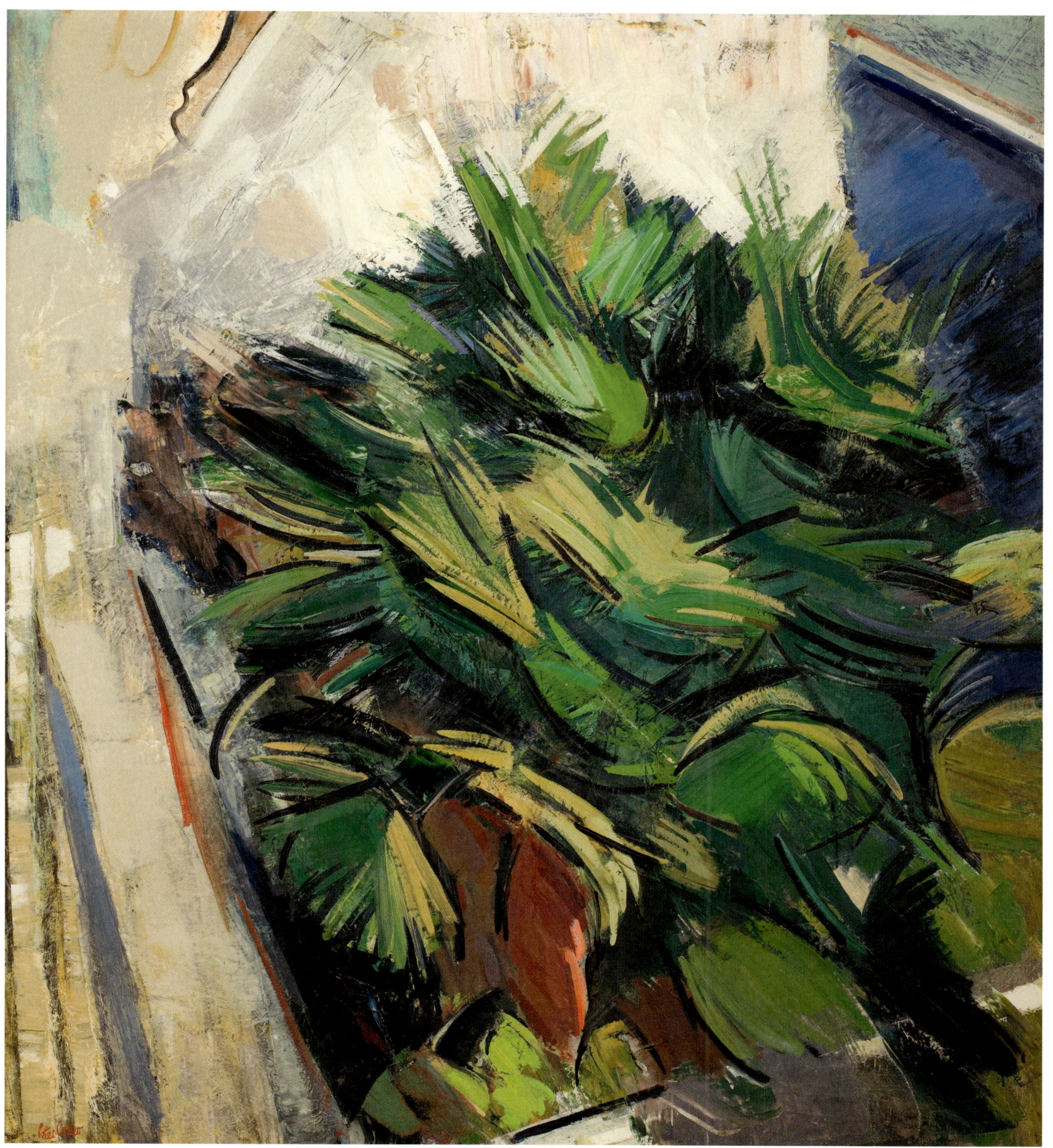

18 | 19 | 20 | 21

Aldeburgh, 1985-86

Signed lower right 'Peter Coker'
Pencil and watercolour
38.1 × 55.9 cm | 15 × 22 in

Provenance
Peter Coker

Literature
David Wootton with contributions by John Russell
Taylor and Richard Humphreys, *Peter Coker RA*
(Chris Beetles Ltd, 2002), cat. rais. SB No. 20, p. 168.

Exhibitions
2005, London, Piano Nobile, *Peter Coker RA*,
Sketchbook No. 20, no. 11, p. 25, col. ill., pp. 30-31.

This quartet of works, *Aldeburgh*, *Cap de la Chèvre*, *Drumrunie*, and *Forêt de Landévennec*, constituted part of Coker's sketchbook number 20 that he worked on throughout 1985 and into 1986. The sketchbooks were fundamental to Coker's practice: he painted or drew in situ and then used the sketchbook works as the stimulus for oil paintings that were created subsequently in his studio. The sketchbooks themselves could be taken apart and the sheaths presented as works in their own right.

Predominantly recognisable locations appear in these four sketchbook works as Coker continued to uncover fresh inspiration on each return, rejuvenated by intimate familiarity with an environment. Aldeburgh, the beach in Suffolk that Coker first discovered in the early 1960s, is seen here from a decidedly modernist viewpoint. The scene, overlooking the shoreline dotted with boats, is bisected by a vertical pillar that jarringly severs the uninterrupted horizontal sweep across the vista. Audierne, another of Coker's haunts and one that pre-dated Aldeburgh, also features, in *Cap de la Chèvre*. Working in watercolour in both *Aldeburgh* and *Cap de la Chèvre*, Coker alternates between light washes of muted browns and greys for an overcast, unassuming British beach and translucent washes and flourishes of rich purples, mosses and mandrakes for the more animated scene of the French coast.

A monochrome ink wash work presents a new location, that of Drumrunie in Badenscallie, North West Scotland. Coker and his wife visited Badenscallie in 1985 for the first time, staying with close friends Colin and Maggie Ellis following the death in March of that year of their only child, Nicholas. Badenscallie is crofting land, remote and bleak, with scrub-covered mountains falling away steeply to the sea and numerous islands dotting the coastline. In *Drumrunie*, the viewer looks through a tangle of undergrowth and spindly trees to a low mountain in the distance, dark clouds scudding overhead. From 1985 onwards, Coker returned often to Scotland. In 1987 he encountered for the first time the sight of salmon nets drying, a motif that proved critical to his work for the remainder of the decade.

Not straying far from familiar territory, the final work in the quartet, *Forêt de Landévennec*, depicts a lone monumental tree in the Landévennec Forest situated in inland Brittany. This sketchbook work is a watercolour study for the oil painting, *Forêt de Landévennec* [cat. 22] of the following year, and the remarkably exact correlation between the two is an illuminating insight into Coker's working process.

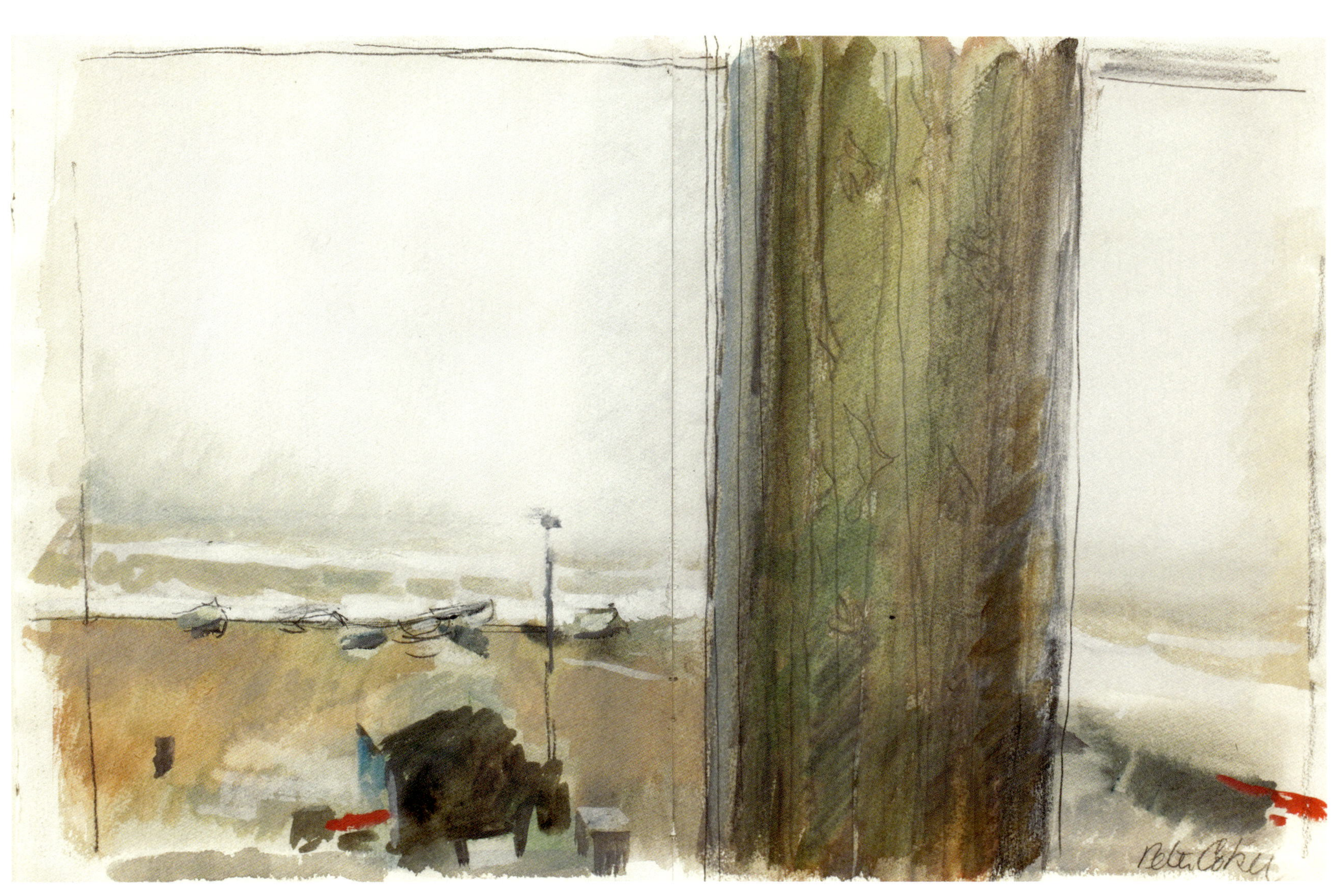

18 | **19** | 20 | 21

Cap de la Chèvre, 1985-86

Signed lower right 'Peter Coker'
Watercolour on paper
38.1 × 55.9 cm | 15 × 22 in

Provenance
Peter Coker

Literature
David Wootton with contributions by John Russell
Taylor and Richard Humphreys, *Peter Coker RA*
(Chris Beetles Ltd, 2002), cat. rais. SB No. 20, p. 168.

Exhibitions
2005, London, Piano Nobile, *Peter Coker RA*,
Sketchbook No. 20, no. 9, p. 25.

18 | 19 | **20** | 21

Drumrunie, 1985-86

Signed lower left 'Peter Coker'
Ink wash on paper
38.1 × 55.9 cm | 15 × 22 in

Provenance
Peter Coker

Literature
David Wootton with contributions by John Russell
Taylor and Richard Humphreys, *Peter Coker RA*
(Chris Beetles Ltd, 2002), cat. rais. SB No. 20, p. 168.

Exhibitions
2005, London, Piano Nobile, *Peter Coker RA*,
Sketchbook No. 20, no. 18, p. 25.

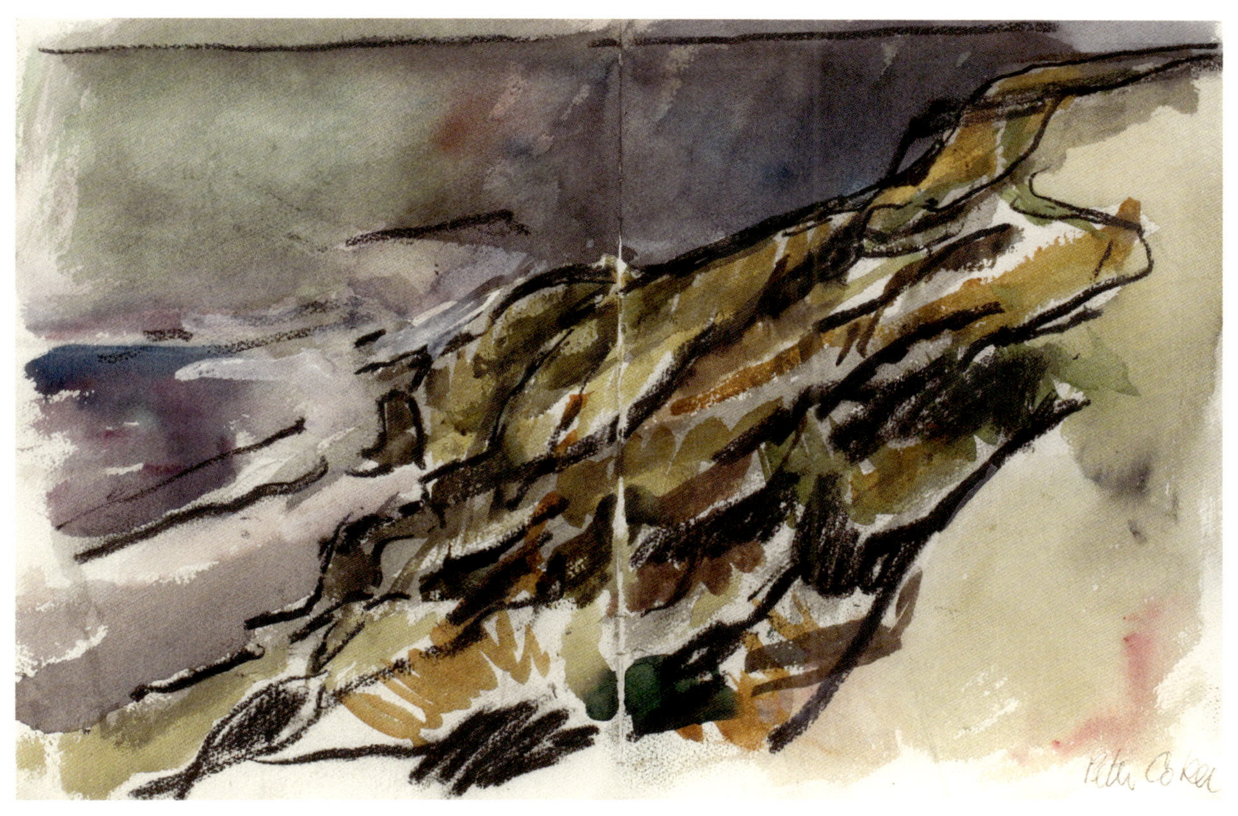

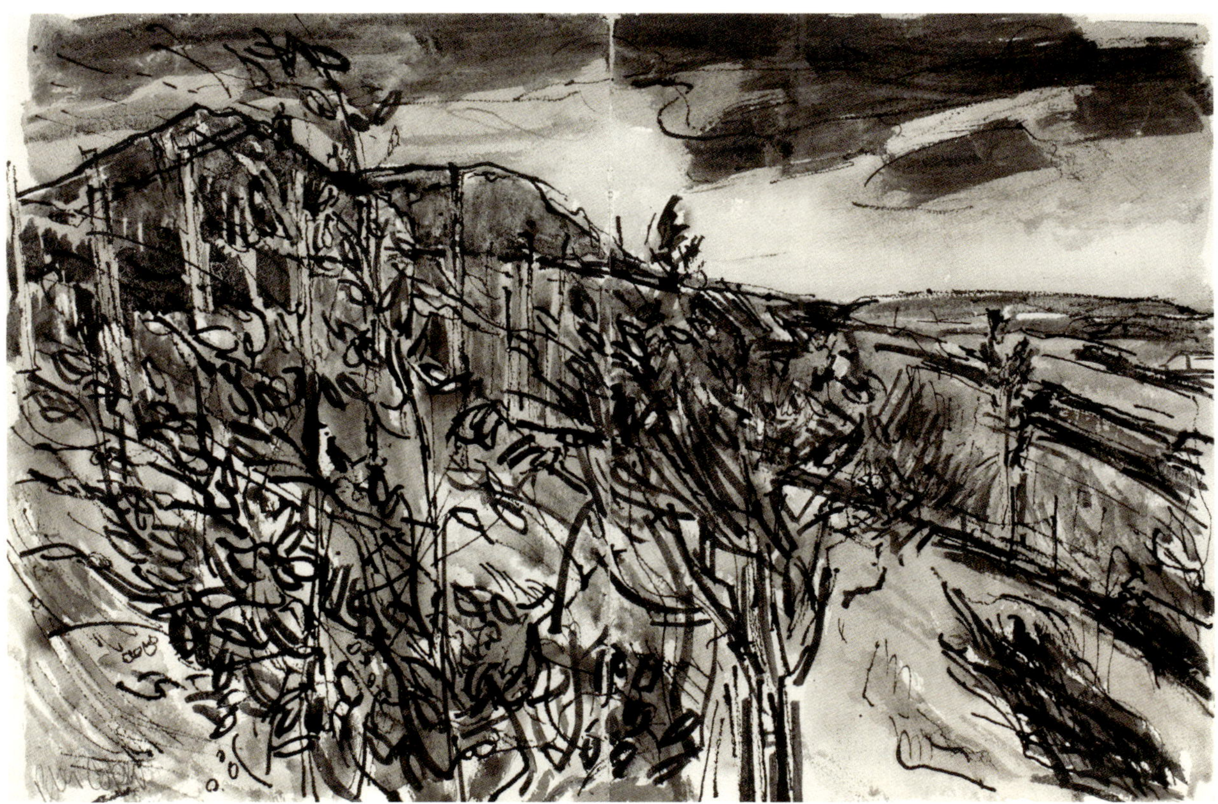

Forêt de Landévennec, 1985-86

Watercolour
38.1 × 55.9 cm | 15 × 22 in

Provenance
Peter Coker

Literature
David Wootton with contributions by John Russell
Taylor and Richard Humphreys, *Peter Coker RA*
(Chris Beetles Ltd, 2002), cat. rais. SB No. 20, p. 168.

Exhibitions
2005, London, Piano Nobile, *Peter Coker RA* ,
Sketchbook No. 20, no. 8, p. 25.

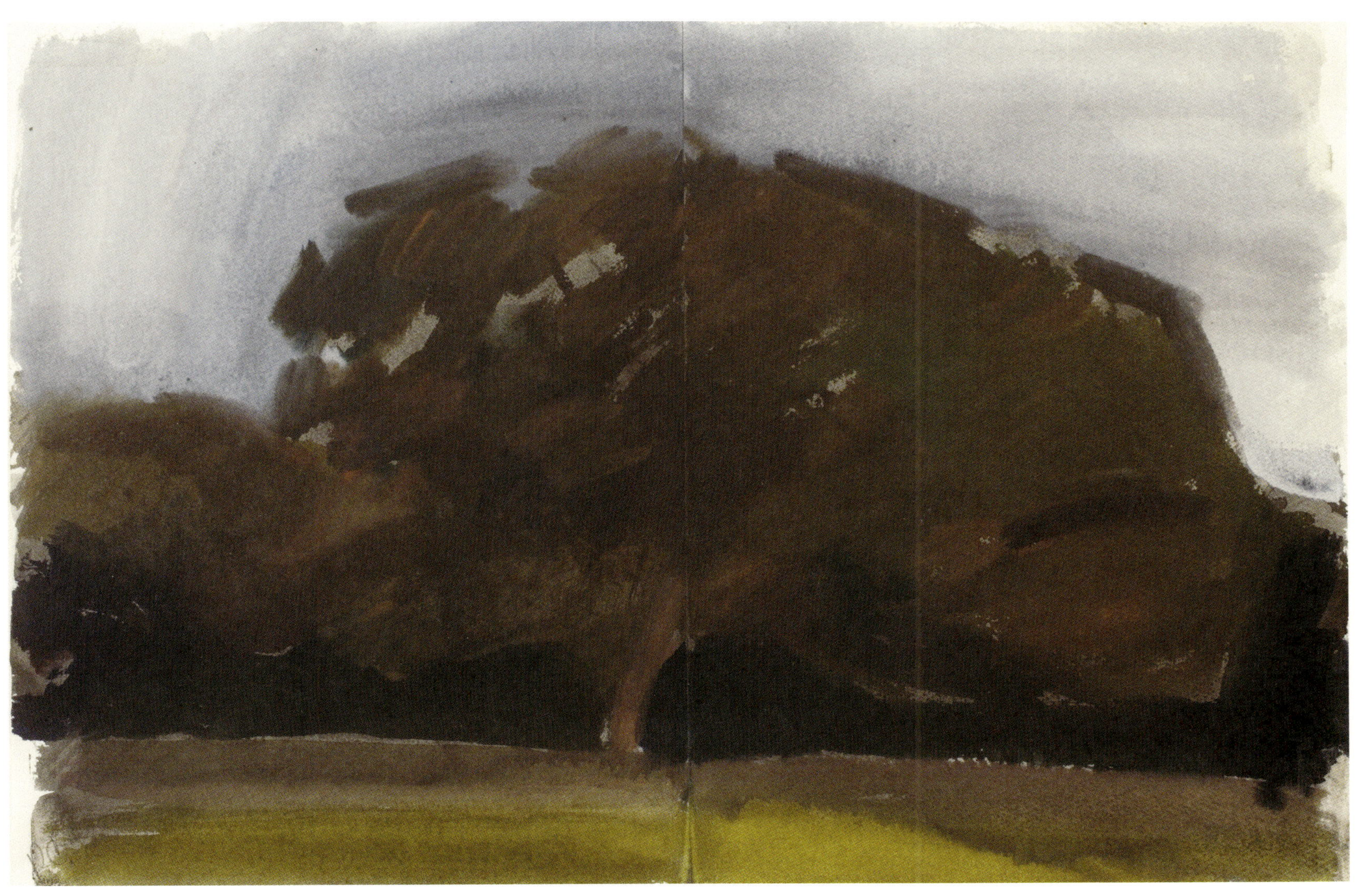

22

Forêt de Landévennec, c.1986

Signed lower right 'Peter Coker'
Oil on canvas
91.4 × 121.9 cm | 36 × 48 in

Provenance
Mr and Mrs Christopher Dunn

Literature
David Wootton with contributions by John Russell Taylor and
Richard Humphreys, *Peter Coker RA*
(Chris Beetles Ltd, 2002), cat. rais. no. 497, p. 137, col. ill., p. 137.

Exhibitions
1986, London, Royal Academy, *Summer Exhibition*, no. 529.
1989, Lancaster, Ohio, Ruthven Gallery, *Classically British,
The Enduring Appeal of English Painting.*

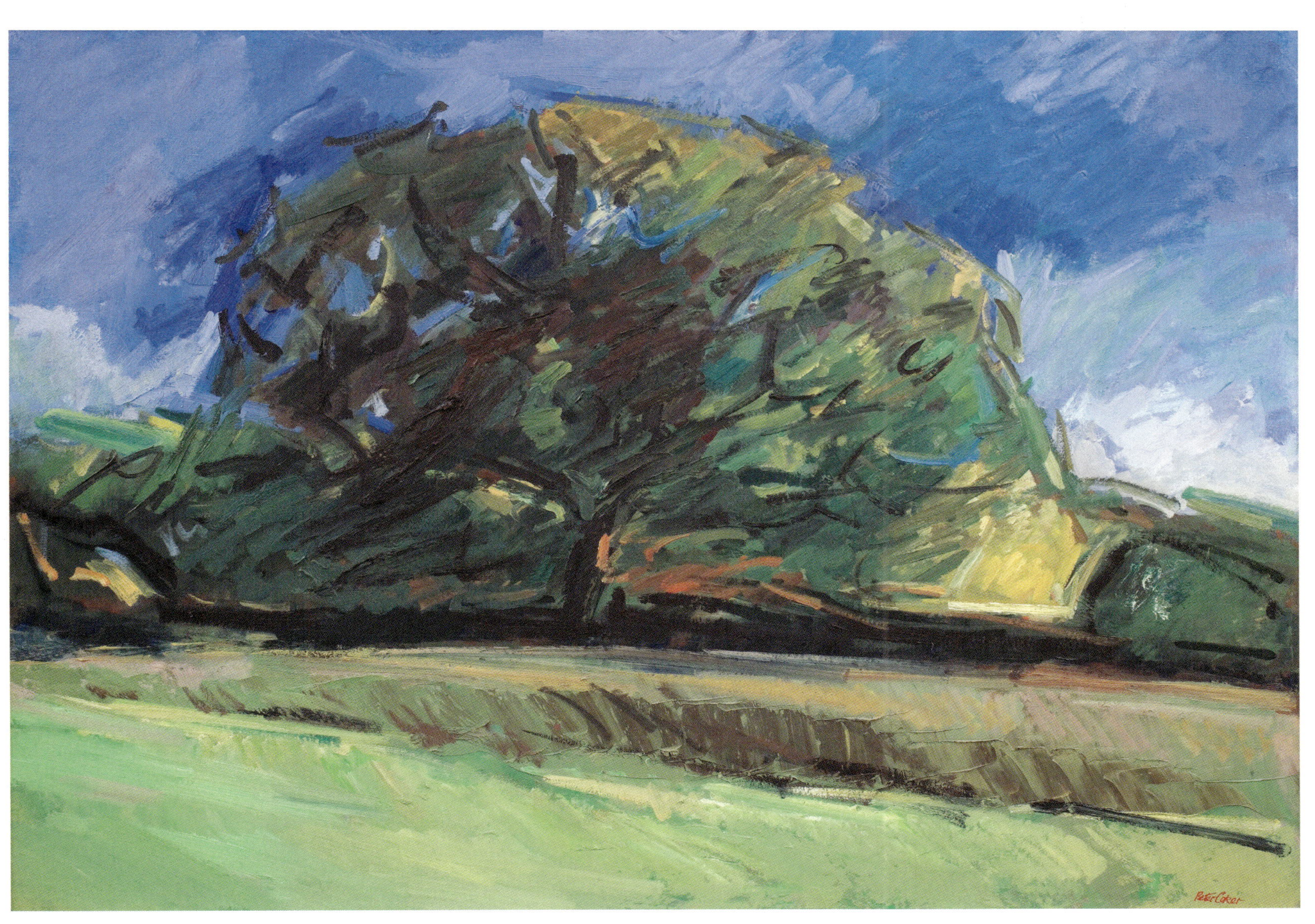

Forêt de Landévennec, c. 1986, first exhibited at the Royal Academy summer exhibition in 1986, depicts the woodlands surrounding Landévennec, a village on the far western Crozon peninsula in Brittany, famed for its ancient abbey, small harbour, and luscious ancient forests. The watercolour study that precipitated the oil painting, *Forêt de Landévennec* [cat. 21], was painted the year previously, though quite possibly from memory as there is no record of Coker visiting France in 1985. It is notable that at this stage in his career, Coker potentially disregards the habit of a lifetime of turning to nature for a subject and instead looks inward, to his imagination or store of memories.

In *Forêt de Landévennec*, a magnificent lone tree extends over an expanse of long grass. Behind, the low-level forest runs the width of the composition but this singular tree, with a presence attributable to great age, is situated apart from the woodland. Throughout his life, Coker was drawn to individual trees, focusing in on such examples as early as *Tree I*, c. 1957 [cat. 6]. In *Forêt de Landévennec* the immense canopy of this tree, rising uninhibited and unconstricted by other trees or shrubs, must have enticed Coker. With a palette and handling process akin to the earlier *The Palm, Château Garden* [cat. 17], it is evident that the effect of southern France profoundly altered Coker's perception of Brittany, where previously he had revelled in a landscape both tempestuous and foreboding. Golden yellow mixed in with the greenery of the boughs intimates the fall of bright sunshine and the occasional overlaying of blue onto the tree suggests glimpses of sky as gusts of wind disturb the branches. The majestic bearing of this tree is recreated on a monumental scale by Coker, its compelling presence epitomising "the dramatic and elemental" that made the landscape Coker's constant muse.[31]

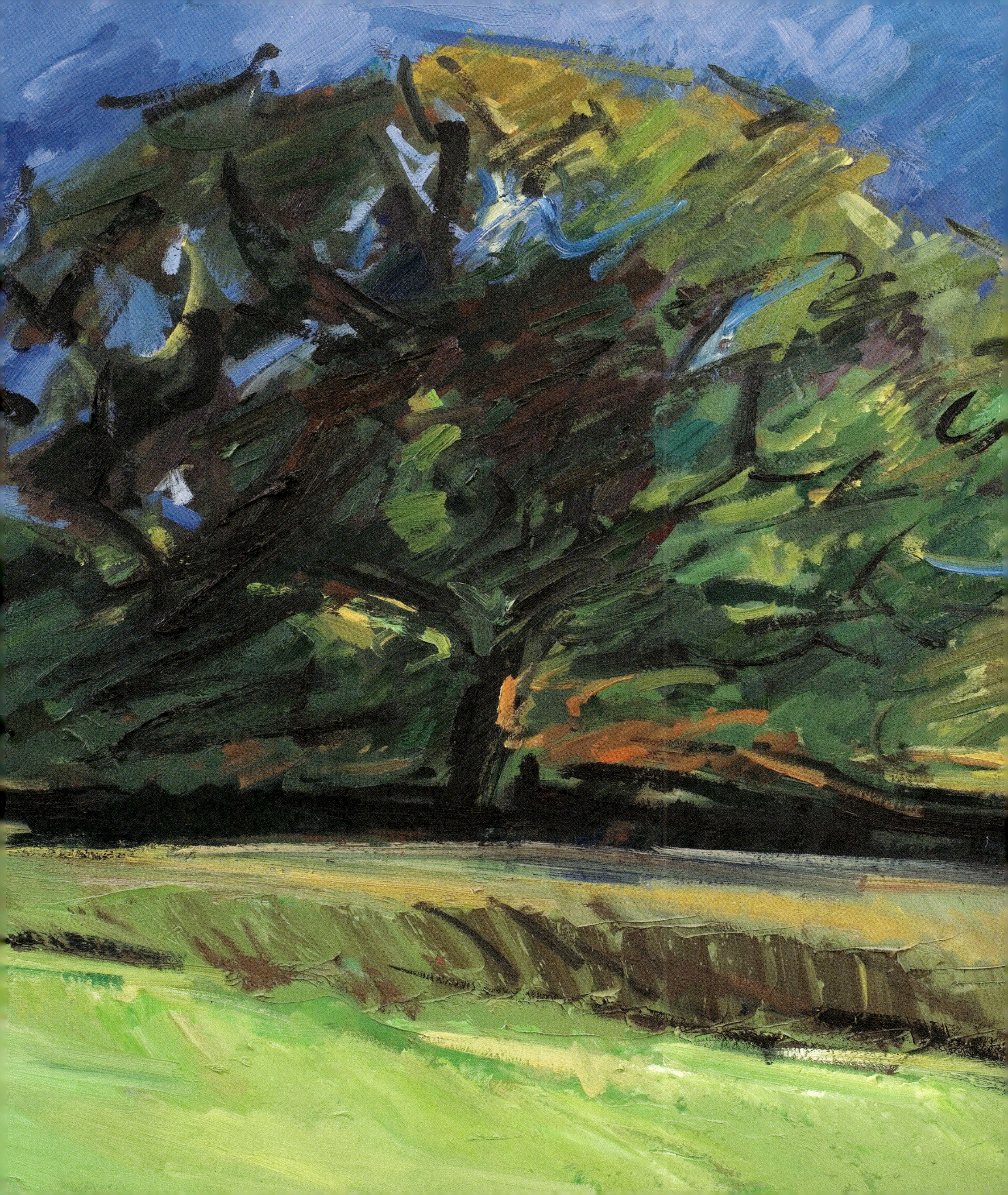

ENDNOTES

1   A. Lambirth in conversation with Peter Coker, 'Peter Coker: A Search for
      Identification', *The Artist's and Illustrator's Magazine* (Issue 36, September 1989),
      p. 16.

2   A. Lambirth, p. 14.

3   A. Lambirth, p. 16.

4   J. Hyman, *The Battle for Realism: Figurative Art in Britain During the
      Cold War 1945-1960* (The Paul Mellon Centre for Studies in British Art,
      New Haven and London; Yale University Press, 2001), p. 119.

5   F. Gore, 'Introduction', *Peter Coker RA: A retrospective exhibition organised
      by the Victor Batte-Lay Trust* (ex. cat. The Minories, Colchester, 1972-73),
      no page nos.

6   A. Lambirth, p. 16.

7   A. Lambirth, p. 14.

8   A. Lambirth, p. 16.

9   A. Lambirth, p. 16.

10   A. Lambirth, p. 14.

11   A. Lambirth, p. 14.

12   A. Lambirth, p. 14.

13   A. Lambirth, p. 16.

14   F. Gore, no page nos.

15   A. Lambirth, p. 16.

16   N. Coker, 'Introduction', *Peter Coker: Paintings & Drawings of the Butcher's Shop*
      (ex. cat., publisher unidentified, 1979), no page nos.

17   J. Russell Taylor quoted in D. Wootton, *Peter Coker RA*
      (Chris Beetles Ltd, 2002), p. 67.

18   A. Lambirth, p. 16.

19   P. Coker quoted in D. Wootton, p. 61.

20   A. Lambirth, p. 16.

21   A. Lambirth, p. 16

22   A. Lambirth, p. 16.

23   F. Gore, no page nos.

24   A. Lambirth, p. 16.

25   D. Wootton, p. 71.

26   D. Wootton, p. 51.

27   A. Lambirth, p. 16.

28   F. Gore, 'Peter Coker', *Peter Coker RA: New Works* (ex. cat. Abbot Hall
      Art Gallery, Kendal; Redcliffe Press Bristol, 1992), p. 13.

29   A. Lambirth, p. 16.

30   A. Lambirth, p. 16.

31   A. Lambirth, p. 16.

BIBLIOGRAPHY

Coker, N., 'Introduction', *Peter Coker: Paintings & Drawings of the Butcher's
Shop* (ex. cat., publisher unidentified, 1979).

Gore, F., 'Introduction', *Peter Coker RA: A retrospective exhibition organised
by the Victor Batte-Lay Trust* (ex. cat. The Minories, Colchester, 1972-73).

Gore, F., 'Peter Coker', *Peter Coker RA: New Works* (ex. cat. Abbot Hall Art
Gallery, Kendal; Redcliffe Press Bristol, 1992), pp. 13-14.

Humphreys, R., *Treasure Island: British Art from Holbein to Hockney*
(ex. cat. Fundación Juan March, 2012).

Hyman, J., *The Battle for Realism: Figurative Art in Britain During the Cold
War 1945-1960* (The Paul Mellon Centre for Studies in British Art, New
Haven and London; Yale University Press, 2001).

Lambirth, A., in conversation with Peter Coker, 'Peter Coker. A Search for
Identification', *The Artist's and Illustrator's Magazine* (Issue 36, September
1989), pp. 14-17.

Lambirth, A., 'Introduction', *Peter Coker RA: A Juxtaposition*
(Paul Holberton, 2004).

Lambirth, A. and Etter, C., *A monographic exploration of Peter Coker's 1958-9
'Sunflowers'* (Piano Nobile Publications, 2012).

Packer, W., 'Peter Coker at Piano Nobile', *Peter Coker RA*
(ex. cat. Piano Nobile Publications, 2005).

Packer, W., 'Introduction', *Peter Coker: Working Drawings and Sketchbooks
1955-1988* (ex. cat. Fitzwilliam Museum, Cambridge, 1989).

Vann, P., *Face to Face: British Self-Portraits in the Twentieth Century*
(Sansom & Company; Piano Nobile Publications).

Wootton, D., with contributions by J. Russell Taylor and R. Humphreys,
Peter Coker RA (Chris Beetles Ltd, 2002).

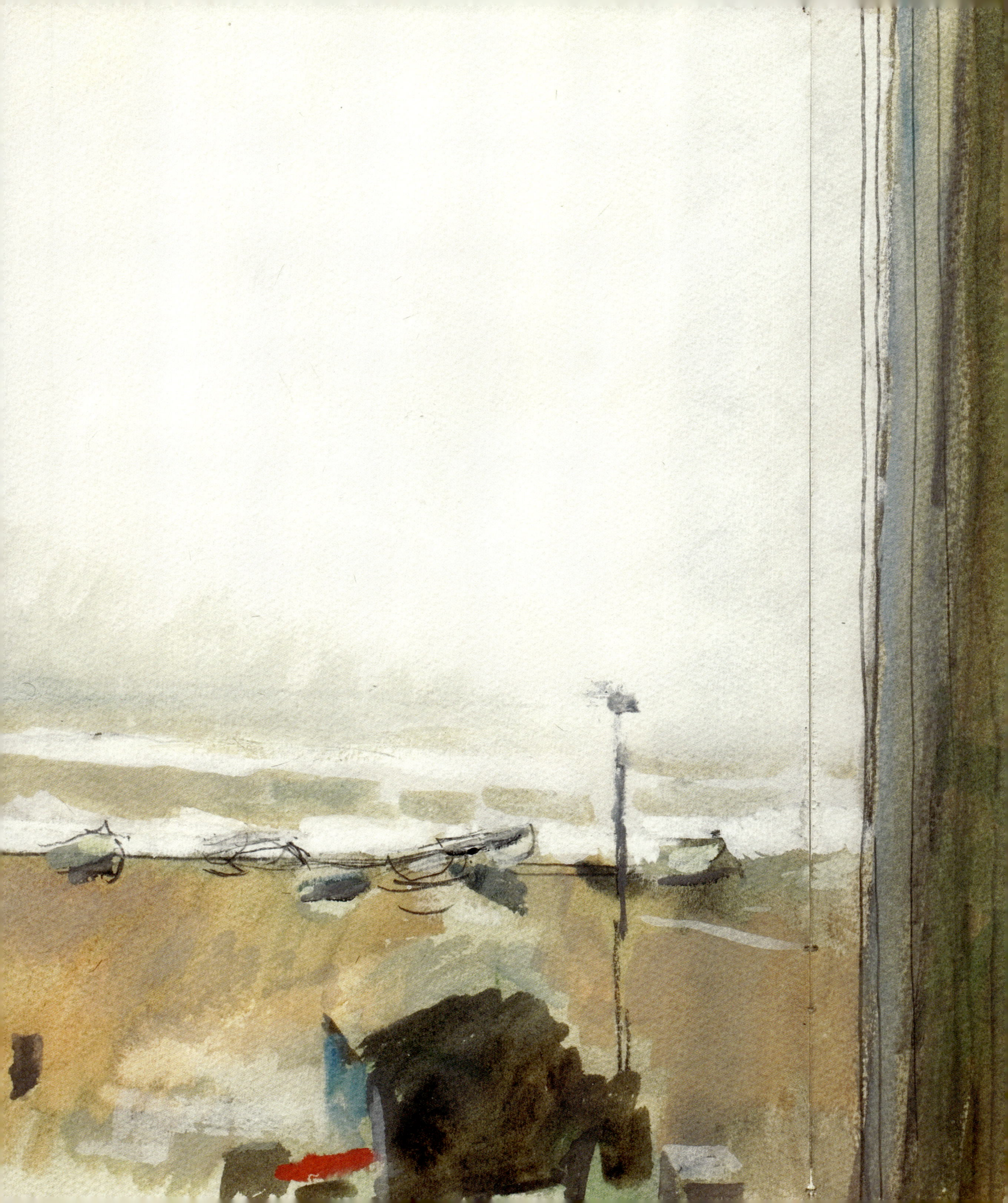

CHRONOLOGY

1926   Peter Coker born July 27th, London (only child).
        Moved to 1 Moyers Road, Leytonstone.

1937   Moved to Maxwelton, Havering-atte-Bower, Essex.

1940   Worked under his father as an assistant at Kerland & Haskin.

1941-43   Studio assistant at Oldham's Press, Covent Garden.
        Attended St. Martin's School of Art and the Central School of Art.

1943-46   During WWII served in the Fleet Air Arm. Later moved to the
        Education Corps, teaching art and allied crafts.

1947-50   Full-time student at St. Martin's in the painting department.

1947   Met Vera Crook, his future wife.

1949   First trip abroad to Italy (3 months). Met with Vera in Paris.

1950   Royal Academy Summer Exhibition; first exhibit *Still Life*.
        Italy with Vera.

1950-54   Studied in the Painting School of the Royal College of Art.

1951   March 31st, married Vera. Returned to 1 Moyers Road, at that time
        still owned by his father.
        Won Royal Scholarship at the RCA.
        Mevagissey, Cornwall with Vera, RCA sketch club prize for
        Landscape China Clay Pits, St. Austell.

1952   February 16th, birth of Nicholas Coker.
        Llanelli, South Wales, made drawings of collieries.

1953   Awarded diploma (ARCA) and a fourth year at the RCA, also a British
        Institution Scholarship.

1953-54   Assisted Rodrigo Moynihan, RCA Professor of Painting.

1954   Made first designs for printed textiles.

1955   Began regular part-time teaching at St. Martin's. Briefly taught
        History of Art and Architecture at Haberdasher Aske's School and
        painting at Ealing College of Art.
        Fontainebleau, Barbizon, Fécamp and Étretat.

1956   First regular use of sketchbooks.
        Zwemmer Gallery, London first one-man exhibition. Associated by
        critics with Kitchen Sink painters.
        Étretat, Quimper and Audierne.
        Devon with Vera and Nicholas.

1957   Passed driving test. All painting trips from this time by car.
        New Forest, first motor trip, with Vera and Nicholas.
        Étretat and Audierne with Vera and Nicholas.
        Zwemmer Gallery, London; one-man exhibition.

1958   Italy and France, including first visit to the South of France,
        with Vera and Nicholas.

1959   Zwemmer Gallery, London; one-man exhibition.
        First of a series of medical problems. Diagnosed with Cushing's
        Syndrome.
        Adrenalechtomy operation at Middlesex Hospital.

1961   Mount Snowdon, Llanberis, Capel Curig and Pembrokeshire with
        Vera and Nicholas.

1962   Became a visiting teacher in life painting at Colchester School of Art.
        Moved to The Red House, Mistley.

1964   Zwemmer Gallery, London; one-man exhibition.

1965   Elected Associate of the Royal Academy (ARA).
        Brittany and the foothills of the Pyrenees with Vera and Nicholas.

1967   Malham, Yorkshire with John Nash.
        David Murray Stewardship at the Royal Academy, for two seasons,
        supervising students in various locations in England and Scotland.

1968   Magdalene Street Gallery, Cambridge; one-man exhibition
        (drawings).
        Stable Gallery, Ufford, Suffolk; one-man exhibition (drawings).

1969   Stone Gallery, Newcastle upon Tyne; one-man exhibition (pastels).
        Ostend, first of many visits.
        Began experimenting with etching techniques.

1970   Thackeray Gallery, London; one-man exhibition.
        Skye with John Nash.

1972   Elected Royal Academician (RA).
        Mouthier-Haute-Pierre, in the Jura.
        Thackeray Gallery, London; one-man exhibition.
        Mollans-sur-Ouvèze, in the Côte de Ventoux, and Aurel with Vera.
        Retrospective: The Minories, Colchester; Victoria Gallery, Bath;
        The Morley Gallery, London and The Mappin Art Gallery, Sheffield.

1973   Leicester Fine Art Gallery; one-man exhibition.
        Mouthier-Haute-Pierre, Sault, Illiers-Combray and Paris.

1974   Thackeray Gallery, London; one-man exhibition.
        Ceased teaching at St. Martin's and began part-time at the City
        and Guilds of London School of Art at the invitation of Roger
        de Grey who had just been appointed Principal.
        Lastours with Vera.

1975   Thackeray Gallery, London; one-man exhibition.

1976   Arts Council Award
        Published *Etching Techniques*.
        Thackeray Gallery, London; one-man exhibition.
        Gravelines.

1977   Bargemon, near Grasse, first of many visits.

1978   Thackeray Gallery, London; one-man exhibition.
        Chelmsford and Essex Museum; retrospective.
        Sault and Bargemon with Vera.

1979   Touring Retrospective: *Paintings and Drawings of the Butcher's Shop*
        University of Liverpool; Carlisle Museum and Art Gallery; Doncaster
        Museum and Art Gallery; Atkinson Art Gallery, Southport; Royal
        Academy of Arts, London.
        Poole Fine Art, Ampthill; retrospective (etchings).
        Bargemon with Vera (two visits).

1980   Paris and Belgium with Vera.
        Bargemon, and first visit to the Hanbury Gardens, La Mortola,
        Italy with Vera.
        Gallery 10, London; one-man exhibition.

1981	Étretat, Vaucottes and Fécamp with Vera.
	Bargemon and Mouthier-Haute-Pierre with Vera.
1982	Greece with Vera.
	Wrote obituary for *The Times* on former teacher and fellow academician, Vivian Pitchforth.
	Gallery 10, London; one-man exhibition.
1982-85	Villa Clos du Peyronnet near Menton, with Vera.
	The Forgotten Fifties; Graves Art Gallery, Sheffield and touring. (Peter Coker rated this exhibition highly).
	Gallery 10, London; one-man exhibition.
1985	March 22nd, death of Nicholas Coker.
	Resigned from the City and Guilds.
	Gorse Bush presented to the Tate in Nicholas's memory.
	Badenscallie, Ross-shire, first of many visits with Vera.
	Wrote obituary for *The Times* on his former teacher and fellow member of staff at St. Martin's, James Stroudley.
1986	Gallery 10, London; one-man exhibition.
	Bargemon with Vera (last visit).
1987	Badenscallie with Vera.
1988	Produced six self-portrait studies, entitled *Le Peintre au Travail* based on a Seurat drawing of the same name in Philadelphia Museum of Art.
	Royal Academy of Art, London; *Exhibition Road. 20th Century Painters from the Royal College of Art*.
	Gallery 10, London; one-man exhibition.
	Christchurch Mansion, Ipswich; *An Artist in Focus*. Works of Peter Coker owned by the Borough.
1989	Retrospective: *Working Drawings and Sketchbooks 1955-1988*. Fitzwilliam Museum, Cambridge.
	Gallery 10, London; *Drawings and Watercolours 1955-1989*.
1990	Suffered serious heart attack.
	Sketchbook drawings used to illustrate the fine wine list for Barwell & Jones.
	Flying Colours Gallery, Edinburgh; one-man exhibition.
	Suffered another serious heart attack and a debilitating stroke.
1991	The Mayor Gallery, London: *The Kitchen Sink Painters*.
	Varengeville and Étretat with Vera.
	Flying Colours Gallery, Edinburgh; one-man exhibition.
	Mayor Gallery, London; *Textile Design in the 1950s*
	James Hyman lecture at Tate; *British Realists, Bratby, Coker and Others*.
1992	Le Havre with Vera.
	Menton with Vera.
	Touring retrospective: *Peter Coker Landscapes 1955 – 1991*.
	Abbot Hall Art Gallery, Kendal; Royal Academy of Art, London; Tullie House, Carlisle; Christchurch Mansion, Ipswich.

1995	Villa Costermano, Bardolino, with Vera.
1998	Menton with Vera.
	Awarded Honorary Fellowship of the Royal Society of Painter-Printmakers (HRE).
	Menton with Vera (last visit).
1999	Lake Bolsena, Orvieto with Vera.
2000	Château Cordeillan-Bages, Pauillac with Vera.
	Watermill Antiques, Nayland: retrospective.
	Paris with Vera to see Courbets in the Musée d'Orsay.
2001	Paris with Vera once again to see the Courbets in the Musée d'Orsay.
	Bologna with Vera to visit the Morandi house and museum at the invitation of the Curator.
2002	Began to paint again after a gap of ten years. Produced the *'Parisian Suite'* of etchings and the paintings of Paris in nine months.
	Chris Beetles Gallery; *Peter Coker, R.A. A retrospective exhibition of work from 1954 to 1992*.
	Publication of *Peter Coker R.A. Biography and Catalogue Raisonné* by David Wootton and John Russell Taylor, to accompany the retrospective exhibition.
2003	Publication of *Peter Coker R.A. New Work 2002* with an introduction by Frances Spalding, to accompany the exhibition of Parisian works at Gainsborough House, Sudbury.
	To Paris with Vera to visit, at their request, the curators of the Bibliothèque Nationale de France and the École des Beaux-Arts.
2004	Royal Academy of Arts; *Peter Coker R.A. Recent Work*. The Parisian works as shown at Gainsborough's House.
	Publication of *Face to Face: British Self Portraits in the Twentieth Century*, with chapter devoted to Peter Coker.
	Publication of *Peter Coker R.A. A Juxtaposition 2004* with an essay by Andrew Lambirth, to accompany the exhibition at the Graves Art Gallery, Sheffield of the Parisian works together with the early Coker pictures in the permanent collection of the City of Sheffield. (11th December 2004 – 5th March 2005).
	December 16th Peter died.
2005	Memorial display, Tate Britain.
	Piano Nobile; *Peter Coker RA (1926-2004)*, 14 April – 7 May.
	Published catalogue with introduction by William Packer; 32 works exhibited, 19 illustrated.
2012	Publication of Nobile Folio, *A monographic exploration of Peter Coker's 1958-9 'Sunflowers'; set alongside an introductory essay by Andrew Lambirth and 'Meditations' by Carrie Etter* by Piano Nobile Publications
2017	Piano Nobile, *Peter Coker: Mind and Matter*, 5 April - 9 May.

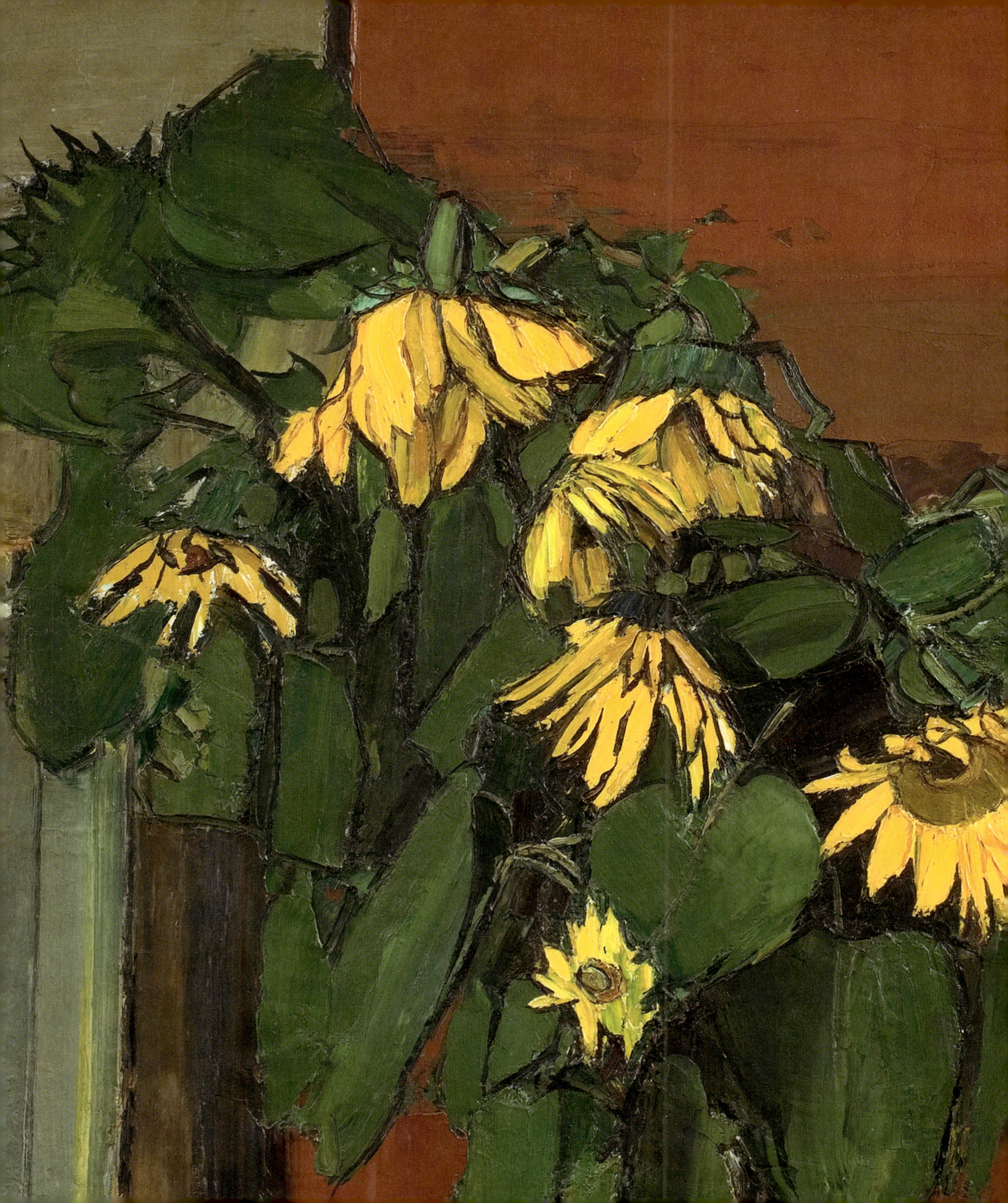

COLOPHON

First published to accompany the exhibition

PETER COKER
MIND AND MATTER

Piano Nobile Publications No. XLIV 2017
ISBN: 978-1-901192-46-9

Editor
Matthew Travers

Foreword
Richard Humphreys

Text
Julia Fischel

Design
Graham Rees Design

Print and Binding
Graphius

Photography
Colin Mills

Index
Elizabeth Wiggans

Acknowledgments
Piano Nobile wishes to extend our sincere gratitude to all those
who helped in putting together this exhibition.

Distributed by Casemate Group
10 Hythe Bridge Street, Oxford, OX1 2EW
casemategroup.com

No part of this publication may be reproduced in any form
whatsoever without the prior permission of the publishers.

Piano Nobile specialises in Modern and Contemporary British and
International works of art. The gallery also represents a select stable
of contemporary artists and artists' estates. Established in 1985,
Piano Nobile provides expert advice for individuals, corporations
and institutions on appraisals, acquisitions and dispersals. With a
discerning curatorial vision, the gallery has established a reputation
for authoritative exhibitions and publications under the gallery's
imprint, Piano Nobile Publications.

Figure 1: p. 12
Nicolas de Staël (1914 – 1955)
Composition 1950, 1950
Tate, London © Tate, London 2015

Figure 2: p. 20
Dead Hare on Table, 1955
Arts Council Collection, Southbank Centre, London
© The artist's estate

Figure 3: p. 26
The Gorse Bush, 1957
Tate, London © Tate, London 2015

Figure 4: p. 30
Sunflowers, 1961
Pallant House Gallery, Bequest of Mrs Vera Coker
in memory of Peter Coker (2014)
© Estate of Peter Coker

Figure 5: p. 38
Nicolas de Staël (1914 – 1955)
Composition 1951, 1951
Private Collection / Photo © Christie's Images /
Bridgeman Images

Figure 6: p. 46
Étretat, 1955
Piano Nobile © The artist's estate

Front Cover
Cat. 5, Still Life with Fish, 1957 (detail)

Inside Front Cover
Cat. 4, Dead Hare, c. 1955

Inside Back Cover
Cat. 1, Ferndale, Rhondda, 1952

Frontispiece
Cat. 13, Tunstall Forest I, 1964 (detail)

Opposite Contents Page
Peter Coker, 1995. Photo by James Hunkin
© Royal Academy

Opposite Foreword
Cat. 17, The Palm, Château Garden, 1979-80 (detail)

Page 8
Cat. 11, Seascape, 1959 (detail)

Page 63
Cat. 18, Aldeburgh, 1985-86 (detail)

Page 67
Cat. 7, Sunflowers, 1958-59 (detail)

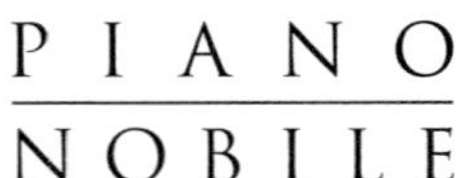

PIANO NOBILE | ROBERT TRAVERS WORKS OF ART LTD
129 Portland Road | London W11 4LW | +44 (0)20 7229 1099
info@piano-nobile.com | piano-nobile.com